DICKENS'S WOMEN

DICKENS'S WOMEN

His Great Expectations

ANNE ISBA

continuum

Published by the Continuum International Publishing Group

The Tower Building	80 Maiden Lane
11 York Road	Suite 704
London	New York
SE1 7NX	NY 10038

www.continuumbooks.com

First published 2011

British Library Cataloguing-in-Publication Data
A catalogue record for this book is available from the British Library.

ISBN: HB: 978-1-4411-0720-6

Library of Congress Cataloging-in-Publication Data
A catalog record for this book is available from the Library of Congress.

Typeset by Fakenham Prepress Solutions, Fakenham, Norfolk NR21 8NN
Printed and bound in Great Britain

'The old unhappy feeling ... pervaded my life ... as undefined as ever, and addressed me like a strain of sorrowful music faintly heard in the night ... the happiness that I had vaguely anticipated, once, was not the happiness I enjoyed, and there was always something wanting.'

Charles Dickens, *David Copperfield* (1849–50)

'Why is it that ... a sense comes always crushing on me now, when I fall into low spirits, as of one happiness I have missed in life, and one friend and companion I have never made.'

Charles Dickens to John Forster (4 February 1855)

'One must love something. Human nature is weak.'

Charles Dickens, 'His Boots', *Somebody's Luggage* (1862)

Contents

List of illustrations

Credits: images 1, 2, 5 and 7 are reproduced courtesy of the Dickens Museum, Doughty Street, London; images 3, 5, 6 and 8, are reproduced courtesy of the National Portrait Gallery, London.

Foreword

Two hundred years after his birth in 1812, many facets of Charles Dickens remain an enigma, not least his perception of women. Dickens was a man who craved a love so unconditional that the yearning was unlikely to be satisfied in this world; a man in thrall to a vision of womanhood so idealized that it was incompatible with everyday domesticity; a man in pursuit of a passion he hoped would transform his existence.

Such aspirations were almost certainly doomed to fail. Dickens's unrealistic expectations made for a messy emotional life but informed much of what went into his writing.

There is something more to our interest in the private lives of great men than the mere desire to pry into other people's personal affairs. A great writer, for example, represents a special concentration both of purpose and of sensibility. He is more conscious than other people of the things that are going on in his time, and he is more articulate about them. He is driven to formulate more clearly some attitude towards the world that he lives in. But the works that he gives to the public do not tell the whole of his story, for they must always be artificial arrangements in the interest of ideal values. The real struggle of the ideal with the actual can only be seen at close range in the relationships and vicissitudes of the man's own life.[1]

So wrote the American critic Edmund Wilson. Dickens's sometimes tortured inner life detracted nothing from the genius of his work, Wilson added, which made it strange that die-hard Dickens continued to imagine, as a model of sound middle-class character,

a man so relentlessly harrowed by violent internal conflicts as Dickens seems plainly to have been and so notoriously unhappy in his domestic life, who had been brought by his worldly success as well as by his devastating genius to a position where there was little to deter him from gratifying his inclinations.[2]

It did not aid Dickens's emotional development that success came to him so early. At a relatively young age he became accustomed to command respect for his writing; perhaps he also came to believe that because he was phenomenally gifted, he was also always right. As his friend and biographer John Forster put it:

His early sufferings brought with them the healing powers of energy, will, and persistence, and taught him the inexpressible value of a determined resolve to live down difficulties; but the habit, in small as in great things, of renunciation and self-sacrifice, they did not teach; and, by his sudden leap into a world-wide popularity and influence, he became master of everything that might seem to be attainable in life, before he had mastered what a man might undergo to be equal to its hardest trials.[3]

If he failed to achieve his objectives by any other means, reinvention or outright denial were often Dickens's resort in the pursuit of self-justification and the maintenance of his public image.

This book seeks to examine some of the effects that Dickens had on some of the women to whom he was close in his life. Dickens cannibalized his own life, and his observations of the lives of others, to feed his art. It is not within the scope of this book to map the characteristics of the real women in Dickens's life onto the female characters in his novels. Establishing such correspondences is complex and subjective, and has been done extensively elsewhere.[4] Certain *leitmotifs* return, of course: the absent mother, the child bride, the young woman acting as surrogate wife to a feckless older man – father, grandfather, or protector; but, by and large, only the most obvious and unavoidable parallels have been drawn.

Every family has its own repertoire of pet names and nicknames, and the Dickens family had more than most. For simplicity, I have called Dickens's wife Catherine in order to distinguish her from her daughter of the same name, whom I have called Katey; and for Catherine's daughter Mary I have chosen the variant Mamey, for consistency of style and to distinguish her from Catherine's younger sister, Mary, who died in Dickens's arms at the age of seventeen and became idealized thereafter as the perfect woman. Another of Catherine's sisters, Georgina – Dickens's housekeeper, hostess and surrogate mother to his children after he separated from his wife – I have called Georgy ('Aunt Georgy' was her principal persona). Dickens's young mistress Ellen Ternan, it appears, was almost always Nelly off-stage; and since it was off-stage that Dickens's relationship with her played out, this is what I have called her. Angela Burdett-Coutts, with whom Dickens collaborated on various philanthropic projects, but most particularly the Urania Cottage hostel for fallen women, was always addressed by Dickens as 'Miss Coutts'. I have done the same. Anything else would have felt impertinent.

To avoid cumbersome and repetitive endnotes, I have not included references to letters from Dickens to his friends and family if the dates are clearly given in the text, and they can therefore be located in the various anthologies of letters listed in the bibliography.

Introduction

'My father did not understand women,' Katey Dickens confided to her friend and biographer, Gladys Storey. Some of the women whose lives were touched by Victorian England's greatest novelist, the writer who called himself the 'Inimitable' one, will have felt that the sentiment was entirely mutual.

Charles Dickens's close relationships with women were always complex, often contradictory, and sometimes manipulative and hurtful. But then, there was about him 'something of the despot seldom separable from genius', wrote his friend and biographer, John Forster.[1] Almost invariably, his relationships with women left him feeling that he was missing something, something undefined that lingered just beyond his grasp. He had a strangely resentful attitude towards his mother Elizabeth who, he believed – and contrary to much of the available evidence – failed adequately to nurture and protect him at a crucial time in his early life, and towards whom, for this, he harboured a lifelong grudge. Then there was his older sister Fanny. Her education was given precedence over his own on the not unreasonable grounds that, short-term, her earning potential was greater than his at a time when the family was in dire financial straits. His being in the blacking warehouse, while his sister was at the music academy and the rest of his family resided in the relative comfort of the Marshalsea debtors' prison, left him feeling permanently undervalued, rejected and, to some extent, abandoned.

1

His first serious sweetheart was Maria Beadnell, whose parents thought the young reporter, amusing though he was, not really good enough for their daughter and discouraged the attachment, a move they would live to regret; her reappearance into his life in middle age would precipitate a crisis from which there was no return.

After his rejection by the Beadnells, he took up with the pretty but ineffectual Catherine Hogarth, whom he married in good faith just as he was about to become famous, but who failed to keep up with his success and was put aside, boring, fat, frumpy and intimidated, in middle age.

Catherine's young sister Mary joined the Dickens household as companion to her sister shortly after their marriage; she died unexpectedly in Dickens's arms, aged seventeen, after which she remained idealized as the perfect virgin, with whom no real-life woman could compete.

A second sister-in-law, Georgy, came to replace Mary and help run the household at the age of fifteen; she became indispensable to Dickens. When Catherine was cast aside, Georgy opted to stay on with him, jeopardizing her reputation at that time and sacrificing the rest of her life to act as his housekeeper, hostess, secretary and surrogate mother to her own sister's children – and, after his death, as guardian of the Dickens image.

After her parents' separation, his second daughter Katey was driven by her father's unbearable behaviour at home into the arms of an unsuitable, sickly and possibly homosexual husband, Charles.

There was Dickens's friend, the benefactress Angela Burdett-Coutts, the richest woman in Britain after Queen Victoria, for whom he managed philanthropic projects, particularly the

Urania Cottage House for Fallen Women. His relationship with her was perhaps the most uncomplicated in Dickens's very complicated life.

And then, just as his mid-life crisis was taking hold, there came into his life the young actress Nelly Ternan, a girl no older than his own daughters. Dickens met her when he was forty-six and she was eighteen; she almost certainly became his mistress and they probably had at least one child – a son – born in France, who died in infancy.

Throughout his life, Dickens had a preoccupation with groups of sisters like his own: the Beadnells (sisters of his first love), the Hogarths (sisters of his wife) and the Ternans (sisters of his last love); and a compulsion, almost, to recreate situations in which he could reprise his childhood role of the responsible male in charge of vulnerable females.

As Dickens became increasingly famous and celebrated, he reinterpreted (and possibly exaggerated) elements of his early life in the context of the important man he had become; and his growing sense of entitlement (accompanied perhaps by his desire to control the course of events, reinventing himself as required) made him wonder why he had not been appreciated sooner by those nearest to him. Perhaps his daughter Katey was even more prescient when, following a conversation with Dickens just days before he died, she voiced her opinion on her father's very public and unkind separation from her mother. They had talked until three o'clock in the morning, she said. 'He said he wished he had been "a better father – a better man".'

Katey, very like Dickens in her impetuous creativity, was both his father's greatest fan and his sternest critic: 'He was a wicked man,' she concluded, 'but I loved him for his faults.' To take away his faults would have been impossible, for they made him 'the uncanny genius' that he was.[2]

Dickens had a touch of the narcissist about him, and for such personalities it is important that other people admire and acknowledge them and enhance their sense of self; unless they do that, they serve no great purpose.

Throughout his life, Dickens harboured a sense of missing something, of true happiness eluding him, lurking round the next corner. He craved the unconditional love that probably only a mother could give – and she hadn't, he felt. However much he achieved, it was never quite enough. Like his young orphaned hero Oliver Twist, Charles Dickens always wanted more.

CHAPTER ONE

Mother

Late one winter's night in 1812, naval petty officer John Dickens, aged 27, and his wife Elizabeth, 22, returned home to their cottage in Mile End Terrace, Portsmouth, after dancing the evening away at a ball held at the Beneficial Society's Hall in Rope Walk, Portsea. They were a good-looking, easy-going pair; a pleasant, carefree young couple who enjoyed life, were hospitable and fond of society – albeit inclined to live somewhat beyond their means.

The Portsea ball would be their last dance for a while. Shortly afterwards, on 7 February, in the front bedroom on the first floor of their little terraced house, Elizabeth Dickens gave birth to their first son. It was a couple of days after the ball, rather than a couple of hours as Elizabeth boasted; for she was proud, to the point of exaggeration, of her image as a woman who took everything in her stride.[1] The boy was a brother for the Dickens's infant daughter Fanny (1810–48) and the second of eight children, six of whom would survive into adulthood.

In 1812, the Prince of Wales, the future George IV, took over as Prince Regent, following the declared insanity of his father, George III; the Luddites continued to wreak havoc, within the vital textile industry in particular, destroying machinery

5

wherever possible as a protest against the social disruption brought about by the Industrial Revolution. Abroad, Napoleon was planning the launch of his devastatingly ill-fated invasion of Russia; and the United States was about to declare war on Britain: those hostilities would continue until 1815. It was an interesting time in which to be born.

Three weeks after his birth, young Dickens was baptized Charles John Huffam at nearby St Mary's Church: Charles after his maternal grandfather, John for his father, and Huffam in honour of an old family friend, sail-maker and chandler Christopher Huffam, who travelled down from London to stand godfather to the boy.[1]

Strictly speaking, having a grandson named after him was more of a privilege than Charles Barrow – father of Elizabeth Dickens – deserved. The young couple's early married life (they wed in 1809) had been overshadowed by scandal when Barrow, Chief Conductor of Monies at the Navy Pay Office – where his son Thomas and John Dickens both worked – was charged with long-term embezzlement. He admitted his guilt, blaming ill-health and the demands of a large family, but fled to the Isle of Man before he could be called to account.

Charles Dickens's grandparents on his father's side were more solid. His grandfather, William, was butler to John Crewe MP, later Lord Crewe, of Grosvenor Street, London and Crewe Hall, Cheshire. His grandmother, Elizabeth (née Ball), had been in service to Lady Blandford, of Grosvenor Square, London and, on her marriage, became housekeeper to the Crewe family. Sadly, William Dickens died four years into the marriage, leaving behind two sons, William and John – Charles Dickens's father. His widow was retained by the kindly Crewes until she was of an age to be pensioned off. Within the Crewe household,

Dickens's mother, Elizabeth

she was renowned for her story-telling skills, with which she delighted all her employers' grandchildren when they visited.

The Crewes were also kind to the fatherless Dickens boys. It was they who secured for young John a position as clerk in the Navy Pay Office, which was how he met Thomas Barrow. Barrow joined the office at the same time as John. The two young men became friends; John met Thomas's sister Elizabeth, fell in love, and married her, despite some initial resistance from her family.

Elizabeth's experience of her father's irresponsible approach to money management may have inured her to the profligate ways of her dear husband, 'D'. There is no suggestion of anything untoward – such as gambling or excessive drink – that might, long-term, have depleted the family finances. But, if it is true that the case of Mr Micawber, in *David Copperfield*, reflected more than a little of John Dickens's own predicament, it was more the gradual accumulation of debt – incurred by living just slightly above one's means for a protracted period – that proved their downfall. 'Annual income twenty pounds, annual expenditure nineteen ninety six, result happiness,' Mr Micawber advised; 'Annual income twenty pounds, annual expenditure twenty pounds and six, result misery,' he warned. It was a concept that Dickens understood well; it was not one that his parents practised.

Perhaps one reason that John Dickens lived beyond his means was because he had developed a sense of entitlement, growing up as he did on the fringe of the wealthy Crewe family; and that, accustomed to being surrounded by the good things in life – although not acquired through the efforts of his own family – he expected to continue to enjoy them. A sense of entitlement also ran through his son Charles's life.

In 1815, John Dickens was transferred from the Navy Pay Office at Portsmouth to London, where he spent two years. By now, the household included Elizabeth Dickens's young widowed sister, Mary Allen, whose late husband's pension helped keep the family finances afloat. Then, in 1817, John Dickens was posted to Chatham. Charles was five years old. He came to regard the Chatham period as the golden time of his childhood, the happiest years of his entire life; it was also to this time that he attributed his growing compulsion to observe and make mental notes of people and events. For this, the town was the ideal location.

Chatham was established as a Royal Dockyard in the reign of Elizabeth I, and many hundreds of ships were launched from there over the next three centuries. It was a garrison town as well as a dockyard, with the addition of prison hulks anchored on the river Medway. It was a place of bustle, activity and excitement, with neighbouring Rochester with its great cathedral providing extra gravitas. John Dickens would take young Fanny and Charles with him on the official boat when he was doing business along the river; he would take them to the local theatre, and to the Mitre Inn, where he would lift Charles onto the table to display his own precocious poetic skills, while Fanny played the piano. It was here that Charles's life-long love of 'theatricals' was born.

There was, however, little formal education in the early years. Elizabeth Dickens taught her two eldest at home. She was a natural and enthusiastic teacher, instilling in them a love of reading and even a little Latin on the side. Or at least she did until the demands of a growing brood made that impractical. Charles and Fanny were then sent to a school run by their next-door neighbour, William Giles, a young Baptist minister, who recognized and encouraged young Charles's eager intelligence and fertile imagination. It was he who first called his young pupil 'the Inimitable', a soubriquet that Dickens cherished all his life. Dickens never forgot this teacher's kindness.

Siblings came along at a steady rate. In all, Dickens had four younger brothers: Alfred Allen, who was born in 1818 and died the same year, Frederick William (1820–68), Alfred Lamert (1822–60) and Augustus (1827–58). And he had at least three sisters: Frances Elizabeth (Fanny, 1810–48), Letitia Mary (1816–93) and Harriet Ellen (1819–22). Only Charles and Letitia survived beyond the age of forty-eight.

There may have been a fourth sister, the significance of which should not be underestimated.[2] An advertisement in the *Morning Chronicle* announced the birth of a daughter on 18 September 1818 to Mrs John Dickens, at Chatham. The only Dickens sibling known to have been born around this time was Harriet, who was baptized on 3 September 1819 and died in early childhood. Could it be that a child – possibly a frail one, at that – would not be baptized for a full year? This seems an excessive delay; Charles and his brother Alfred Allen, the only two for whom both birth and baptism dates are certain, were both christened shortly after birth. Other accounts have Harriet being born and baptized on the same day – 3 September 1819 – quite normal, if a child were sickly (although it was smallpox that took her in 1822).

So Dickens may have had two sisters born within a year, both of whom died young. There was no legal requirement, until 1837, to register either births or deaths; the absence of concrete evidence is not, therefore, conclusive. Dickens was too young to understand much of his brother Alfred's death; he was just two years old when Alfred died aged six months. But he was around ten when Harriet – and possibly another sister – died. If young Dickens did, indeed, lose two sisters within a short period of time, it must have created an intense sense of grief at so young an age, prompting an overwhelming longing, in adult life, to recreate the happy sibling configurations of early childhood, in life as in fiction. For the death of the first Alfred left Charles as the only brother of three (or possibly four) sisters until the birth of Frederick in 1820. No surprise, then, that in adult life he felt drawn – domestically, socially and emotionally – to situations in which he could recreate the role of the principal male responsible for a trio of vulnerable women.

His preoccupation with the concept of groups of sisters also found its expression in one of his more bizarre *Sketches by Boz*, 'The four sisters', which described just such a group: a quartet of spinsters, courted and apparently wedded corporately by a single suitor, until only pregnancy reveals the true bride.

In 1821, Charles's widowed Aunt Mary married surgeon Matthew Lamert. As she left the household, the eldest of Lamert's three sons, James, came to live with them instead. A keen play-goer, he encouraged Charles's growing passion for the stage, taking him to see plays and building for him a toy theatre.

But the golden years at Chatham were drawing to a close. In 1822, John Dickens was recalled to London, on a reduced income, and the family's financial affairs were slipping into increasing disarray. It was a difficult time altogether. Within a short period, little Harriet – and possibly another sister – died, as did his aunt Mary, in Ireland. The following year, Charles also lost his closest childhood confidante when his sister Fanny was accepted as a boarder at the newly founded Royal Academy of Music in Hanover Square.

Charles was deeply fond of Fanny, his kind and 'constant companion' as a child and the inspiration for many of the 'sisterly' characters in his novels, including Florence Dombey (*Dombey and Son*), Agnes Wickfield (*David Copperfield*), Esther Summerson (*Bleak House*), Biddy (*Great Expectations*) and even Nancy (*Oliver Twist*). But he was dismayed at the difference in their education.

Fanny's studies at the music academy cost 38 guineas a year – about one-tenth of her father's basic income. Charles's education, on the other hand, had effectively ceased with the move to London; his only lessons now were those he learned in the school of life as he roamed the streets of the capital on errands for his father, or just whiled away the time recording the sights, sounds and smells of the city, particularly its seedier neighbourhoods.

The investment in Fanny's future, but not his own, can hardly have failed to rankle. It was not an unreasonable choice; Fanny's musical talents were more obvious at that stage than her brother's latent literary ones, making her a potentially more profitable earner. And that proved to be the case, in the short term: even after John Dickens was no longer able to continue paying Fanny's fees, the girl was able to obtain some work as a teacher at the academy. But still Charles felt he was the subject of benign neglect. He loved his father, who was kind and easy-going, perhaps to a fault, since he commented that John Dickens appeared

in the ease of his temper, and the straitness of his means, to have utterly lost at this time the idea of educating me at all, and to have utterly put from him the notion that I had any claim upon him, in that regard, whatever.[3]

As the family sank deeper and deeper into debt, Elizabeth Dickens – ever the optimist – had the idea of opening a school to help pay the bills. It was a last-ditch attempt. But she had the support of her husband, and the encouragement of Charles Huffam. Huffam had business contacts in the East Indies, and Elizabeth was persuaded that she might prevail upon him to recommend her establishment to families wanting to send their children to be educated in England. Suitable premises (more expensive than their existing house) were found. A brass plaque advertising 'Mrs Dickens's Establishment' was screwed to the front door. Prospectuses were printed and distributed by young Charles throughout the neighbourhood. But no enquiries ever came; not locally, nor from the East Indies. The failure of the school – and the investment that had been made in the project – was the final straw that would tip the family finances into the abyss, a fact which Dickens appears to have blamed almost exclusively on his mother's blind optimism.

In the meantime, James Lamert, who had originally been destined for the Army, had taken a post as a manager in Warren's Blacking Warehouse, a boot polish factory on the Strand. He offered Charles a job, working in his own little cubby-hole and receiving an hour's instruction from Lamert during the midday break. He was aware of the family's straitened circumstances – as his aunt by marriage, Elizabeth Dickens might even have made the first approach to him herself. Yet it was, said Dickens, 'an evil hour, as I often bitterly thought'.

James Lamert, the relative who had lived with us in Bayham Street, seeing how I was employed from day to day, and knowing what our domestic circumstances then were, proposed that I should go into the blacking warehouse, to be as useful as I could, at a salary, I think, of six shillings a week. I am not clear whether it was six or seven. I am inclined to believe, from my uncertainty on this head, that it was six at first and seven afterwards.[4]

The offer was accepted 'very willingly' by his parents. They could not have been more satisfied 'if I had been twenty years of age, distinguished at grammar school, and going to Cambridge'.[5] The next Monday, he went down to the warehouse 'to begin my business life'. 'It is wonderful to me how I could have been so easily cast away at such an age,' he told Forster.

It is wonderful to me that, even after my descent into the poor little drudge I had become since we came to London, no one had compassion enough on me – a child of singular abilities, quick, eager, delicate, and soon hurt, bodily or mentally – to suggest that something might have been spared, as certainly it might have been, to place me at any common school. Our friends, I take it, were tired out. No one made any sign.[6]

The factory was in a decaying, tumble-down old house by the river, overrun by rats that swarmed relentlessly through the cellars and up and down the rotting stairs. Dickens's job was to cover the pots,

first with a piece of oil-paper, and then with a piece of blue paper; to tie them round with a string; and then to clip the paper close and neat, all round, until it looked as smart as a pot from an apothecary's shop. When a certain number of grosses of pots had attained this pitch of perfection, I was to paste on each a printed label; and then go on again with more pots.[7]

Lamert's arrangement whereby Charles would work in his own recess, and have an hour's teaching midday, failed to materialize 'through no fault of his or mine', and soon the boy was down in the main workshop with the 'common' boys, one an orphan called Fagin.

No words can express the secret agony of my soul as I sunk into this companionship; compared these every day associates with those of my happier childhood; and felt my early hopes of growing up to be a learned and distinguished man, crushed in my breast. The deep remembrance of the sense I had of being utterly neglected and hopeless; of the shame I felt in my position; of the misery it was to my young heart to believe that, day by day, what I had learned, and thought, and delighted in, and raised my fancy and my emulation up by, was passing away from me, never to be brought back any more; cannot be written. My whole nature was so penetrated with the grief and humiliation of such considerations, that even now, famous and caressed and happy, I often forget in my dreams ... even that I am a man; and wander desolately back to that time of my life.[8]

Two weeks after Charles began work at Warren's, John Dickens was arrested for debt and detained in the Marshalsea prison. The Marshalsea prison opened in 1329 and closed in 1842. It housed political dissidents, free-thinking radical intellectuals and homosexuals. But, most of all, in Dickens's time at least, it was a debtors' prison.

Before the Bankruptcy Act of 1869 abolished debtors' prisons completely, people were routinely imprisoned – sometimes for decades – for owing as little as twenty pounds. When the Fleet prison was closed in 1842, some minor debtors had been there for thirty years.

The insidious practice of charging inmates for their keep while in prison meant that, for some, the debt just kept growing and growing, and the prospect of its ever being discharged kept slipping further and further away. A parliamentary report concluded that, as a result, 300 inmates starved to death within a three-month period in 1729. Even more insidious, perhaps, was the fate of remand ('untried') prisoners who were subsequently found 'not guilty', but who, because of the board and lodging costs incurred while awaiting trial, were transferred directly to the debtors' side of the prison once they were found not guilty.

After her husband was arrested, Elizabeth Dickens stayed on at the family home in Gower Street for a time, while its contents were sold or pawned, before moving into the Marshalsea with her younger children. Fanny was safely ensconced at the music school. Lodgings were found for Charles with a family friend in Camden Town who took in children and, at the age of twelve, he was effectively left to fend for himself. He never got over the trauma caused by the experience, which he relived in *Oliver Twist* (1837–9) and *David Copperfield* (1849–50), the most intensely autobiographical novel that he called his 'favourite child'.

In 1847, when he was 35 and the idea for *David Copperfield* was fermenting, Dickens entrusted to his great friend and first biographer John Forster an autobiographical fragment that described the impact on him of that early experience. Even allowing for the nostalgia and the wisdom of hindsight, it is clear that, just as his father believed the 'sun had set' when he entered the Marshalsea prison, Charles believed his childhood died at Warren's. Most of all, he dreaded going back at night to his lodgings 'and such a miserable blank'. He was too young and childish to manage his own existence, he told Forster, and found it difficult to budget for food.

I do not exaggerate, unconsciously and unintentionally, the scantiness of my resources and the difficulties of my life. I know that if a shilling were given me by anyone, I spent it in a dinner or tea. I know that I worked, from morning to night, with common men and boys, a shabby child. I know that I tried, but ineffectually, not to anticipate my money, and to make it last the week through; by putting it away in a drawer I had at the counting-house, wrapped into six little parcels, each parcel containing the same amount, and labelled with a different day. I know that I have lounged about the streets, unsufficiently and unsatisfactorily fed. I know that, but for the mercy of God, I might easily have been, for any care that was taken of me, a little beggar or a little vagabond.[9]

But, above all, he missed the comfort of family life.

I was never, for one hour, reconciled to [this existence], or was otherwise than miserably unhappy. I felt keenly, however, the being so cut off from my parents, my brothers and my sisters.[10]

Every Sunday morning he would collect Fanny from the music school and they would walk together to spend the day at the Marshalsea. One Sunday, he 'remonstrated with my father … so pathetically and with so many tears, that his kind nature gave way', and new lodgings were found for Charles, closer to the prison, with a Mrs Roylance in Little College Street. It was only a back attic, overlooking a timber yard, but 'I thought it was a Paradise'. He could now have breakfast and the evening meal with his family, and listen to his mother's wonderful gossipy tales of the fates that had befallen other inmates of the prison. In the Marshalsea, the family had 'no want of bodily comforts'. John Dickens was still drawing his salary, and the family still kept their young maid (an orphan from the Chatham workhouse), who came in daily. Charles commented that 'in every respect indeed except elbow-room, the family lived more comfortably in prison than they had done for a long time out of it', and certainly more happily than Dickens in his lodgings.

A month into his internment, John Dickens obtained a medical certificate to the effect that, because of a 'chronic affection of the urinary organs' he was, in effect, unfit for work and should therefore be pensioned off. This was not a ploy. It would be the very same bladder complaint that proved fatal in 1852.

While John Dickens and family were in the Marshalsea, his mother died. The old lady, who had enjoyed a pension from the Crewe family, had lived soberly and invested wisely. She left most of her money to her elder son William, on the grounds that John had received 'several sums of money from her years previously'. Thanks to this money, William was able to settle his brother's debts; John Dickens was released from the debtors' prison on 28 May 1824 and returned to his old job at the Navy Pay Office, his invalidity pension application still pending. The entire family moved into Mrs Roylance's lodging house for a while, before renting a small house in Somers Town.

Meanwhile Fanny was going from strength to strength at the Royal Academy of Music. Dickens recalls attending a prize-giving ceremony at which his sister received two awards.

I could not bear to think of myself – beyond the reach of all such honourable emulation and success. The tears ran down my face. I felt as if my heart were rent. I prayed, when I went to bed that night, to be lifted out of the humiliation and neglect in which I was. I never had suffered so much before. There was no envy in this.[11]

About this time, the blacking warehouse moved round the corner from the Strand to Covent Garden. Charles had achieved 'great dexterity' in tying up the pots of polish, and he and Fagin had been given a position near the window to take advantage of the light.

We were so brisk at it, that the people used to stop and look in. Sometimes there would be quite a little crowd there; I saw my father coming in at the door one day when we were very busy, and I wondered how he could bear it.[12]

It seems John Dickens could perhaps not bear it, after all, to see his son so humiliated. A disagreement ensued between him and James Lamert, which resulted in Charles losing his job. But the family finances were still precarious and Elizabeth Dickens took it upon herself to call on Lamert and, success-fully, persuade him to offer to take Charles back. Her husband, however, remained firmly against it.

My mother set herself to accommodate the quarrel, and did so next day. She brought home a request for me to return next morning, and a high character of me, which I am very sure I deserved. My father said I should go back no more, and should go to school. I do not write resentfully or angrily, for I know all these things have worked together to make me what I am, but I never can forget, I never shall forget, I never can forget, that my mother was warm for my being sent back.[13]

Charles's resentment towards his mother hardened into a grudge that endured for the rest of his life. As for his parents, they never again spoke of that period in their lives: 'From that hour, until this, they have been stricken dumb upon it.'[14]

Dickens was at Warren's for a year or so – it may have been as much as fourteen months, a long time in the life of a child. Could the experience really have been so bad that it affected his relationship with his mother for ever? Did he blame her failed school scheme (which, at the time, seemed eminently sensible to all concerned) for tipping the family over into irredeemable debt? Perhaps a son simply expects too much of his mother.

In some ways, having independence thrust on him at such an early age was the making of Dickens, as he himself admitted. When his son Edward, 16, was leaving for Australia to join his brother Alfred, Dickens wrote to him: 'I was not as old as you are now when I first had to win my food, and to do it out of this determination; and I never slackened in it since.'[15] His son Sydney was expected to become independent at an even younger age; he was just 13 when he became a naval cadet.

On an emotional level, however, the Warren's experience took away from 12–year-old Dickens the sense of unconditional security that is ideally part of any childhood. Together with the sense that his sister Fanny was valued more highly than him, it left him with a yearning that any future emotional encounter would struggle to satisfy.

He also suffered agonies of shame over his father's impris-
onment for debt and the family's situation of shabby gentility.
George Bernard Shaw, an admirer of Dickens's writing, felt that
this was one of Dickens's handicaps: falling between two classes,
being born into 'a false position as a member of the shabby
genteel class – the class which pretends to gentility without the
means to support its pretension'.[16] As a result, Dickens suffered
from

the special shabby genteel disadvantage of a false knowledge of the
working class based on his childish observation of and intimacy
with domestic servants, who have hardly any class characteristic but
their illiteracy in common with the workers who, in mine, factory,
workshop, and East End quarter, live their own life, obeying the
factory bell at stated hours instead of the drawing-room bell at all
hours, and getting its glimpses of a better life through the imagination
instead of through the keyhole.

In his formative years, Shaw continued, Dickens 'knew as
little of the great world of thought as he did of the great world
of labour'; he was 'not merely ignorant of "the humanities"; he
was absolutely unconscious of them'.[17]

This is a harsh judgement by Shaw; but it does nothing to
minimize the importance of Dickens's childhood experiences
and observations in a wider context, in that life in the raw
alerted him to the real and massive issue of the exploitation and
neglect of tens of thousands of children in Victorian England –
an awareness that found full expression in his writings.

Throughout his life, Dickens was regularly irritated by his
parents' feckless behaviour and their ongoing demands on his
purse; however much money was coming in, they would always
spend that bit more than they had. He tried dispatching them
to Devon, out of the way, an enterprise which proved no great
success. On the other hand, he thought the world of his father

– more so even as he grew older. Nor was he averse to calling on his mother's skills as a homemaker where necessary – to refurbish his bachelor quarters in advance of his marriage, for example.

Precisely why Dickens bore such a lifelong grudge against his mother for the unfortunate one-year interlude in his early life remains something of an enigma. Elizabeth Dickens, like Mrs Micawber, was a loyal and devoted wife who stood by her man through thick and thin. Until the Warren's/Marshalsea period, she seems to have been an attentive and engaged mother, stimulating the imagination of her children as she taught them and encouraging an enquiring spirit. It was she, after all, who visited Warren's regularly while her son was there, while her husband called in once; and it was she who found him, aged 15, his first 'proper' job as a legal clerk, again through contacts of her own.

Mary Weller, who was the family's nursemaid during the Chatham years, described her as 'a dear mother and a fine woman'.[18] In later years, the wife of the physician Robert Davey, at whose Bloomsbury home John Dickens was a resident patient in the period before his death, commented that 'Mrs Dickens does not seem to have foreseen the future celebrity of her son in his childhood'.[19] But, she added, Elizabeth Dickens was a 'thoroughly good-natured, easy-going, companionable' person.

She possessed an extraordinary sense of the ludicrous, and her power of imitation was something quite astonishing. On entering a room, she almost unconsciously took an inventory of its contents, and if anything happened to strike her as out of place or ridiculous, she would afterwards describe it in the quaintest possible manner. In like manner, she noted the personal peculiarities of her friends and acquaintances. She had also a fine vein of pathos, and could bring tears to the eyes of her listeners when narrating some sad events ... I am of the opinion that a great deal of Dickens's genius was inherited from his mother.[20]

Therein, perhaps, lay part of the problem. To become a man, a boy must distance himself from his parents, from his mother in particular; after which, having become a man, he may – if he wishes – return to her. However, if he perceives himself, rightly or wrongly, to have been rejected by his mother, in advance of his rejection of her, this procedural challenge can adversely affect all future relationships with women.

Perhaps, despite his protestations to the contrary, Charles was indeed jealous of Fanny and resentful of the recognition accorded her within the family, feeling himself under-appreciated in comparison. Perhaps he overly anticipated grief and loss, after the death of his siblings. Perhaps he inherited his father's enhanced sense of entitlement. Perhaps he felt so profoundly that his mother had betrayed him, by expecting him to return to Warren's, that he could never forgive her. Perhaps he over-sensationalized his memory of that period, incorporating it into the drama of his fiction, and then reflecting the fiction back as if it had been real life. That would not have been out of character. 'It is always risky … for biographers to take [Dickens's writing] as straightforwardly autobiographical, even though Dickens may have been happy for his readers to interpret them.'[21]

On the other hand, something may have happened during his time at Warren's of which he could not speak – something he thought a mother, so dear to him previously, should somehow have intuited. Was there some exposure to bullying, depravity or crime, perhaps, that scarred the 12–year-old for ever? Dickens, in his books, was always concerned not to give offence with what he wrote. Of his 'autobiographical fragment' he commented: 'It does not seem a tithe of what I might have written, or of what I meant to write.' What was it that he left unwritten? Whatever it was, the ghosts of that experience haunted him forever.

I have never had the courage to go back to the place where my servitude began. I never saw it [the location]. I could not endure to go near it. For many years, when I came near to [it], I crossed over to the opposite side of the way, to avoid a certain smell of the cement they put upon the blacking-corks, which reminded me of what I once was. It was a very long time before I liked to go up Chandos Street [to Covent Garden]. My old way home by the borough made me cry, after my eldest child could speak.[22]

When he entered the blacking factory, Charles was young, sensitive and anxious. Whether it was the awfulness of Warren's, the experiences to which the 'common' lads introduced him, or the absence of his mother, that heightened his anxiety, his view of Elizabeth Dickens as the jolly young woman who told him stories and taught him Latin was gone forever, utterly dissolved at Warren's where he felt she had abandoned him. When he emerged from the warehouse, their relationship could never be the same again. He managed his feeling of nostalgia for what he had hoped for from a mother, and his perceived abandonment, by translating it into active renunciation.

It has often been pointed out that

more mothers died in Victorian fiction than in real life. By presenting so many of his characters as motherless, Dickens was mining a rich seam of contemporary fiction. Without a real-life, workaday, perhaps embarrassing mother such as Dickens had, the author had a blank slate on which the cultural ideal of sentimental maternity could be written, and characters created who desperately sought a suitable object for their affections.[23]

The novel form can use 'maternal absence to invent a deeply emotional and abstract vocabulary of motherhood and family',[24] even, presumably, if that absence is more perceived than real.

George Bernard Shaw observed that all Dickens's boy heroes (and many of his heroines as well) had mothers who failed them by being dead, weak, ineffectual or in one case, fake; the 'maternal' care of boys and men of any age was delegated to surrogates, often daughters, sisters or aunts – mainly childless. Elizabeth Dickens, however, did not fail her son by silliness, death or neglect. On the other hand, Dickens may simply have felt resentful, writing his 'autobiographical fragment' as he did with the benefit of adult insight and a growing sense of entitlement, that his mother had failed to recognize the true potential of the child he once was. The absence of positive middle-class mother figures in Dickens's fiction, Shaw claimed, was 'not a reasoned omission, nor in its manner of execution, a just one'. He maintained that Dickens believed that his mother ought to have suffered increased poverty to preserve in him an essentially false sense of dignity, regardless of the cost to her.

Dickens failed to understand that the family system, particularly among people clinging to appearances with straitened means, sacrificed the woman's life entirely to the struggle to keep her children 'fed, taught, patched and darned'; and that there was no assumption that any degree of delight in her children would make this monstrous obligation a pleasure.

Neither in this nor in any other matter did Dickens ever catch the woman's point of view, or escape from that of the British bourgeois. To him the perfect woman is simply the perfect domestic convenience.[25]

CHAPTER TWO

Lover

In early 1830, when he was just 18 years old and working as a shorthand reporter in the ecclesiastical and family courts known as Doctors' Commons,[1] Charles Dickens fell seriously in love for the first time. The relationship would struggle on for three years. And serious was the word. There was little light-hearted or light of touch in the surviving letters and poems from the young swain to his inamorata.

The object of his affections was Maria Beadnell (1811–86). The youngest of three daughters of George Beadnell (1773–1862), a banker at Smith, Payne and Smith in the City of London, Maria was a year older than Dickens; she was small – Dickens always favoured small women – pretty and coquettish. Nor was she short of other ardent suitors. They included Dickens's friend Henry Austin who later married Dickens's sister Letitia. Dickens became a regular visitor to the Beadnell home, which was 'over the shop' in Lombard Street. He was introduced to the family by another friend, Henry Kolle (1808–81), who was then also in banking (he later moved into stove manufacture) and who married Maria's sister Anne in 1833. By 1831, Dickens was totally infatuated with Maria.

He made no secret of his admiration. For Maria's autograph album he composed an acrostic on her name, believed to be his first literary effort. It is fair to say that the mawkish idealization and precious, dated style of expression in this and other poems written to Maria give little hint of the great writer Dickens would soon become. Perhaps that, in itself, is significant, in that it marks the Beadnell relationship as a rite of passage that radically changed the callow youth into the more resilient man. They are, in any case, all we have. In Maria's album, Dickens wrote:

<u>M</u>y life may be chequered with scenes of misery and pain,
<u>A</u>nd 't may be my fate to struggle with adversity in vain:
<u>R</u>egardless of misfortunes tho' howe'er bitter they may be,
<u>I</u> shall always have one retrospect, a hallowed one to me,
<u>A</u>nd it will be of that happy time when first I gazed on thee.

He wrote another poem in the book, initialled and dated November 1831, entitled *The Devil's Walk*. In it, the Prince of Darkness passes by the Beadnell home and, seeing Maria at the window, this fallen angel is momentarily reminded of the heavenly bliss that once was his.

As the Devil was passing I won't say where
But not far from Lombard Street,
He saw in a window a face so fair
That it made him start and weep.[2]

Clearly unperturbed by Henry Austin's competition for Maria's attention, Dickens also wrote a poem entitled *Lodgings to Let* as a commentary to accompany a watercolour painting in the album by his future brother-in-law. The picture shows 'an open window framed in an attractive setting of brick, woodwork and green shutters. By the window, a handsome

Maria Beadnell, Dickens's first love, sketched by his rival Henry Austin, later his brother-in-law

young woman may be observed busily rinsing a bottle and glasses in a wash tub. Behind the lifted sash a printed notice has been affixed: "Lodgings to let".[3] The poem ran:

Lodgings *here*! A charming place,
The *Owner's* such a lovely face
The Neighbours too seem very pretty

Lively, sprightly and witty
Of all the spots that I could find
This is the place to suit my mind.

Then will I say sans hesitation
This place shall be my habitation
This charming spot my home shall be
While dear 'Maria' holds the key.

About this time, Dickens also wrote a 400–line poem in rhyming couplets, entitled *The Bill of Fare*, describing the characters of the core members of the Beadnell circle that met regularly at Lombard Street. The poem is an imitation of a 1774 work by Oliver Goldsmith (1730–74) called *Retaliation*.[4] In it, Dickens likens each of his characters to some food they might bring to an imaginary dinner party, and then writes for each an imaginary epitaph.

Mr Beadnell, Maria's father, is compared to 'a good fine sirloin of beef/ Though to see him cut up would cause no small grief', and, as to his wife: 'And then Mrs Beadnell, I think I may name/As being an excellent *Rib* of the same'. Of himself (who is not included in the imaginary obituaries), he writes:

And Charles Dickens, who in our Feast plays a part,
Is a young Summer Cabbage, without any heart;
Not that he's *heartless*, but because, as folks say,
He lost his a twelve month ago, from last May!

Moving on to the mock epitaphs, Dickens writes of Maria:

But who have we here? Alas what sight is this!
Has her spirit flown back to regions of bliss?
Has Maria left this world of trouble and care
Because for us she was too good and too fair.

With remarkable prescience, Dickens also creates a mock

epitaph for Maria's best friend, the equally flirtatious Mary Anne Leigh, who would precipitate the end of their relationship.

And Mary Anne Leigh's death I much regret too,
Though the greatest tormentor, that e'er I knew;
Whenever she met you, at morn, noon, or night.
To tease and torment you was her chief delight
To each glance or smile she'd a meaning apply,
On every flirtation she kept a sharp eye.
Though, – tender feelings I trust I'm nor hurting –
She ne'er herself much objected to flirting.
He to each little secret always held the candle,
And I think she liked a small bit of scandal.

In praise of Maria's father, George Beadnell, Dickens wrote:

Here lies Mr Beadnell, beyond contradiction,
An excellent man, and a good politician;
His opinions were always sound and sincere.

If Dickens was thankful for George Beadnell's friendship and hospitality to a struggling young journalist, he was particularly grateful to Mrs Beadnell for introducing him into polite society. His epitaph for her reads:

Here lies Mrs Beadnell, whose conduct through life,
As a mother, a woman, a friend, a wife,
I shall think, while I possess recollection.
Can be summ'd up in one word – *perfection.*[5]

Kind though they were to young Dickens, the Beadnell parents were not keen on him as a suitor for their daughter. He was good company; he was witty, flamboyant, entertaining. But he was not the stuff that good sons-in-law were made of. As yet he was merely a junior reporter at Doctors' Commons. Clearly ambitious, he came nevertheless from a shabby-genteel background with his father, with whom he still lived, having been imprisoned for debt. So the Beadnells whisked Maria back to her finishing school in Paris, and out of harm's way.

Dickens was not to be so easily deterred. In 1831, he had begun working as a reporter for *The Mirror of Parliament*, whose editor was his uncle J. M. Barrow, but he was so fired by the desire to do something that would deeply impress Maria that he returned to his earliest passion: the theatre. In private, he practised his acting skills intensively and, in March 1833, aged 21, he felt brave enough to approach the Covent Garden Theatre, where he secured an audition. His sister Fanny was to go with him as his accompanist. But, when the day came, he was laid low with a terrible cold and facial neuralgia and had to cancel. By the time his audition could be rescheduled for the next season, his career had taken off in a journalistic direction. The stage was forgotten as a professional career option, but putting on 'theatricals' – private, semi-professional and professional – would become from then on a lifelong passion whatever role he played: scriptwriter, actor, producer, director, stage manager, publicist, even builder of scenery. The stage provided the opportunity for Dickens continually to reinvent himself.

At this time, Dickens's sketches were beginning to be accepted for publication, and he had obtained a post as parliamentary reporter on the London daily newspaper the *Morning Chronicle*. He had won, as he said, 'a distinction in the little world of the newspaper'. And he liked it.

Maria Beadnell returned from Paris on holiday some time in the second half of 1832. Her letters to Dickens do not survive, but it would appear from his letters to his friend Kolle, who again acted as go-between in their clandestine correspondence, that it was she, in fact, who sought to re-establish contact with Dickens. Dickens was more than keen to oblige.

In the summer of 1832, Dickens wrote to Kolle, asking him to deliver a letter to Maria:

I trust ... that you will not object to doing me the very essential service of delivering the inclosed as *soon* this afternoon as you can, and perhaps you will accompany the delivery by asking Miss Beadnell only to read it when she is *quite alone* (of course in this sense I consider you as nobody).

The next day, he urged:

As I was requested in a note I received this morning to forward my answer by the same means as my first note, I am emboldened to ask you if you will be so kind as to deliver the inclosed for me when you practise your customary duet this afternoon.

There appear to have been several secret meetings between Dickens and Maria during the winter of 1832–3, after which there was an estrangement which ultimately proved terminal. Dickens expressed himself bewildered by Maria's apparent indifference. Maria complained that Dickens had confided too many intimate details of their relationship to her so-called 'friend', Mary Anne Leigh, the 'tormentor' and 'flirt' of Dickens's earlier poem, *The Bill of Fare*.

Dickens was distraught. He denied all culpability. On 18 March 1833 he wrote to Maria:

Our meetings of late have been little more than so many displays of heartless indifference on the one hand, while on the other they have never failed to provide a fertile source of wretchedness and misery.

He suggested returning to Maria some presents he had received from her; not, he stressed, to hurt her feelings, but because he felt it was inappropriate to keep them, 'and I can only wish that I could as easily forget that I had ever received them'. He spoke of the feeling of 'utter desolation and wretchedness which has succeeded our former acquaintance'. In his own vindication, he felt he could claim for himself

the merit of having ever throughout our intercourse acted fairly, intelligibly and honourably, under kindness and encouragement one day and a total change of conduct the next I have ever been the same. I have ever acted without reserve. I have never held out encouragement which I knew I never meant; I have never indirectly sanctioned hopes which I well knew I did not intend to fulfil. I have never made a mock confidante to whom to intrust a garbled story for my own purposes ... I have done nothing that I could say would be very likely to hurt you ... A wish for your happiness, altho' it comes from me, may not be the worse for being sincere and heartfelt. Accept it as it is meant, and believe that nothing will afford me more real delight than to hear that you, the object of my first and last love, are happy.

Maria remained her cool, heartless self; Dickens remained constant. The affair limped on. In April 1833, three weeks before Kolle married Anne Beadnell, Dickens staged some 'theatricals' at his family's new home in Bentinck Street. Playbills were printed, and both Maria and Mary Anne were invited. In the meantime, information had come to the attention of Dickens's sister Fanny which indicated that Mary Anne Leigh was herself deeply attached to Dickens and that, to further her own cause, she had recounted to Maria a grossly exaggerated account of her intimacy with him. At a meeting between Dickens and Maria in early May, he strongly denied he had ever made a confidant of Mary Anne, whose duplicity he had only just heard of from Fanny. He talked the matter over with Kolle, whose wedding was just a week away, deciding, on reflection, that he should obtain Maria's consent before he wrote a letter of protest to Mary Anne. He enclosed the letter to Maria in one to his friend. 'My dear Kolle', he wrote, as Miss Beadnell is a party concerned and as Mary Anne Leigh's malice in the event of my writing might be directed against her, I have thought it best to ask her consent to my writing at all, which I have done in the enclosed note. You know how I feel upon the subject, and how anxious I naturally am, and I am sure, therefore, you will do all you can for me when I say that I want it delivered immediately. I have lost too much time already.

His letter to Maria, dated 14 May, denounced Mary Anne's behaviour but also blamed Maria for being indiscreet in confiding in her too much. He insisted:

I never by word or deed, in the slightest manner, directly or by implication, made in any way a confidante of Mary Anne Leigh; and never was I more surprised, never did I endure more heartfelt annoyance and vexation, that to hear yesterday by chance that days, even weeks, ago she had made this observation – not having the slightest idea that she done so, of course it was out of my power to contradict it before.

He accused Mary Ann Leigh of interference, 'duplicity and disgusting falsehood'. It was she who had volunteered the information that Maria had confided to her, without reserve, everything that had passed between Dickens and Maria. In proof of which assertion, she gave details. It was his sister Fanny, Dickens added, who had alerted him to the fact that Mary Anne had her own agenda. He requested an immediate reply.

Two days later he received an answer. He wrote back immediately, denying any suggestion that he had paid any attention to Mary Anne, despite her throwing herself at him. He suggested to Maria that she had made two fundamental mistakes:

In the first place, you do not exactly understand the nature of my feelings with regard to your alleged communications with M.A.L.; and, in the next, you certainly totally and entirely misunderstand my feeling with regard to her – that you could suppose, as you clearly do … that I have ever really thought of M.A.L. in any other than my old way, you are mistaken. That she has, for some reason to suit her own purposes, of late thrown herself in my way, I could plainly see, and I know it was noticed by others. For instance, on the night of the play, after we went upstairs, I could not get rid of her. God knows that I have no pleasure in speaking to her or any girl living, and never had.

Dickens continued at length his tedious dissection of the problem created by Mary Anne, before returning to 'the question of what is to be done', that is, whether or not a letter of protest should be sent to the woman. 'You will act as you think best,' Dickens conceded. 'It is too late for me to attempt to influence your decision,' he wrote, adding:

Towards *you* I never had and never can have an angry feeling. If you had ever felt for me one hundredth part of my feeling for you, there would have been little cause of regret, little coldness, little unkindness between us. My feeling on *one* subject was early roused; it has been strong, and will be lasting. I am in no mood to quarrel with anyone for not entertaining similar sentiments, and least of all, dear Miss Beadnell, with you. You will think of what I have said, and act accordingly – Destitute as I am of hope or comfort, I have borne much, and I dare say can bear more.

Maria agreed to Dickens's sending the protest letter to Mary Anne, of which she first made a copy for her own records, as she did in the case of the declaration above.

Maria asked to see Mary Anne's answer, and Dickens, failing to see the minx at work, thought he sensed a note of conciliation and hope, as he communicated to Kolle when sending his reply. It would be the last time he could use his friend as a go-between, since within days he would be married to Maria's sister and therefore, on grounds of propriety, out of bounds for such adventures. 'My dear Kolle', he wrote,

I inclose a very conciliatory note. Sans pride, sans reserve, sans anything but an evident wish to be reconciled, which I shall be most obliged by your delivering.

Independently of the numerous advantages of your marriage, you will have this great consolation, that you will be once and for aye relieved from these most troublesome commissions. I leave the note myself, hoping that it is possible, though not probable, that it may catch you so as to be delivered today.

The 'very conciliatory note' that he enclosed revisited in relentless detail the issue of Mary Anne Leigh's interference in their relationship, before concluding with a profound, forgiving, sincere – albeit ponderous – declaration of total and lasting devotion.

I will allow no feeling of pride, no haughty dislike to making a concili-ation to prevent my expressing it without reserve … I will only openly and at once say that there is nothing I have more at heart, nothing I more sincerely and earnestly desire, than to be reconciled to you … I have no guide by which to ascertain your present feelings and I have, God knows, no means of influencing them in my favour.

I have never loved and I can never love any human creature breathing but yourself. We have had many differences, and we have lately been entirely separated. Absence, however, has not altered my feelings in the slightest degree, and the Love I now tender you is as pure and as lasting as at any period of our former correspondence.

I have now done all I can to remove our most unfortunate and to me most unhappy misunderstanding. The matter now of course rests solely with you, and you will decide as your own feelings and wishes direct you.

Maria remained unmoved. Dickens was heart-broken, but he bore up. As he wrote to Kolle: 'Least said, soonest mended.' The relationship had struggled along for most of its duration. Dickens decided to give up and move on. He was hungry for a relationship that would provide him with some measure of domestic bliss (or at least he thought he was).

In the event, it would be 1845 by the time Maria Beadnell got married, at the advanced (for the time) age of 34, to Henry Louis Winter, a sawmill manager in Finsbury. By this time Dickens – once deemed an inadequate match for their daughter by the Beadnell family – was the father of six and the acclaimed author of seven best-selling novels, the latest of which, *A Christmas Carol*, had established him as the Victorian paterfamilias *par excellence*, the virtual creator of the modern Christmas. Maria Beadnell and her parents must have been kicking themselves.

There was the occasional flutter of contact between the two families. When Maria's brother Alfred died in India, Dickens sent a letter of condolence to the parents, and when Maria's mother died in1849, he wrote a letter of condolence to George Beadnell in which he described 'the sympathy of an old friend in your affliction' and recalled that 'the memory of many old kindnesses bestowed on me when I was a mere boy, rise vividly before me in connection with your melancholy tidings.'

A quarter of a century after their doomed youthful affair ended, Maria would come back into Dickens's life, albeit briefly and catastrophically. It seems that she was the one to make contact. On receiving a letter from her in early February 1855, 'three or four and twenty years vanished like a dream, and I opened it with the touch of my young friend David Copperfield when he was in love,' he wrote. 'Then the three or four and twenty years began to rearrange themselves in a long procession between me and the changeless Past, and I could not help considering what strange stuff all our little stories are made of.'

Before they met again face to face and reality rushed in, she was still Dickens's former 'Angel of my soul'.

In the strife and struggle of this great world where most of us lose each other so strangely, it is impossible to be spoken to out of the old times without a softened emotion. You belong to the days when the qualities that have done me most good since, were growing in my boyish heart … We are all sailing away to the sea, and have a pleasure in thinking of the river we are upon, when it was very narrow and little.

A few days later, on 15 February and now in Paris, Dickens opened his heart up to Maria.

I have always believed since, and always shall to the last, that there never was such a faithful and devoted poor fellow as I was. Whatever of fancy, romance, energy, passion, aspiration and determination belong to me, I have never separated and never shall separate from the hard-hearted little woman – you – whom it is nothing to say I would have died for!

The aim of being worthy of Maria was what had inspired him to make something of himself, Dickens added, and to fight his way out of poverty and obscurity.

Maria Beadnell's reappearance – and the memories it rekindled of this intensely emotional early love affair – was far from being the romantic success Dickens had hoped for, but it would contribute significantly towards precipitating Dickens's middle-life crisis, after which things would never be the same again.

But this was all in the future. The year now was 1833. Charles Dickens was twenty-one years old; he had just had his first short story published in *Monthly Magazine*. His star was in the ascendant and, above all, he was in want of a wife.

CHAPTER THREE

Wife (and her sisters)

Catherine Hogarth was born into a close and well-established family of literati in Edinburgh's elegantly modern 'New Town' on 19 May 1815, making her just over three years younger than Dickens, and nineteen years old when they met. She was the eldest of ten siblings, five of each sex, of whom one – Mary Scott Hogarth – had died in infancy, after which her name (not an uncommon practice at the time) was passed on to the next girl child born. The death of the second Mary, who also died young, would have a profound effect on Dickens's emotional development.

The girls were educated at home by their parents. Their mother, Georgina, was herself well educated. Their father, George Hogarth, was a trained, though unsuccessful, solicitor, and always strapped for cash; but he was also a brilliant musician with an urge to make a career in journalism. To supplement the family finances, he also offered his services as a private tutor in the educational basics: reading, writing, arithmetic and geography. In the case of his daughters, this was supplemented with tutors for piano, singing and dancing lessons, while the boys were sent off to the Continent to improve their French and German.

The Hogarths came to London from Edinburgh via Exeter and Halifax, where George sought to consolidate his journalistic career. In 1834, he took up a position as music and theatre editor at the capital's liberal and influential newspaper, the *Morning Chronicle*. The Hogarths made their home at York Place in Brompton.

In early 1835, Hogarth, now also co-editor of the about-to-be-launched *Evening Chronicle*, invited young Dickens – who had already had sketches published in the *Morning Chronicle* – to contribute a story for the inaugural issue of the newspaper. In the event, twenty of his sketches appeared in the newspaper in the first eight months of the year; in the process, the contacts between Dickens and the Hogarth family flourished.

It is not unfair to say that ambitious young Dickens, not yet famous, was impressed by the Hogarth family's credentials. Rich the Hogarths were not – but then, Dickens's own background was shabby-genteel, with pretensions to gentility but without the means to support it; his debt-ridden father would be a perpetual drain on Dickens's purse.

One of the Hogarths' great attractions for Dickens was that they had more than one link by marriage to Dickens's great hero, Sir Walter Scott.

Charles Dickens and Catherine Hogarth became engaged in the spring of 1835, when they had known each other for just a few months. He was earning enough to be married: a salary of almost £400 a year was quite adequate to support a family by Victorian standards.

Both were eager to be married. Catherine had enjoyed a happy family life during childhood and entered marriage with no expectation other than that this state of affairs would be replicated; Dickens's expectations were more complicated.

Young Catherine Dickens, née Hogarth

If Dickens's letters to Maria Beadnell were characterized by the sense of a callow youth's attachment to his imagined ideal woman, approachable or not, deserving or otherwise, his letters to Catherine Hogarth struck a quite different, more realistic tone. This time, clearly, he felt confident in the attachment of his chosen one – she must have agreed eagerly and early to his proposal – and he addressed her accordingly.

His frequent absences on journalistic business were clearly an issue, even during their engagement, and that issue would only become greater with the passing years. On 14 December 1835, he wrote to her: 'To say that I very much regret being away is, I know, unnecessary, and it is equally useless to say that I am most anxious to get back.'

A few days later, Catherine wrote to complain that his reply to a letter of hers had been 'stuffy and formal'. Dickens replied, on 18 December, assuring her that

if it really were (which I can hardly believe), it was quite unintentional … I am most happy to hear you have not been 'coss' – though I perceive you have not yet subdued one part of your disposition – your distrustful feelings and lack of confidence. However this may be, you may rest satisfied that I love you dearly – far too well to feel what in any one else would have annoyed me greatly.

During their engagement, Dickens infantilized Catherine, calling her not only his 'darling' but also his 'darling Tatie', 'my dearest life', 'dearest mouse', 'dearest titmouse', 'pig', signing off his letters with kisses numbering between ten thousand, several zillions, or, simply, 'an unlimited number'. Yet he was always eager to make it clear to her that his work came first, even if it meant cancelling an evening they had planned to spend together.

On 18 January 1836, he explained his predicament to her:

Young Charles Dickens

If you knew how eagerly I long for your society this evening, or how much delight it would afford me to be able to turn round to you at our own fireside when my work is done, and seek in your kind looks and gentle manner the recreation and happiness which the moping solitude of chambers can never afford, you would believe me sincere in saying that necessity, and necessity alone, induces me to forego the pleasure of your companionship for one evening in the week even.

You will never do me the justice of believing it, however, and all I can do until my book is finished will be to reflect that I shall have (God willing) many opportunities of showing you for years to come how unjust you used to be, and of convincing you then of what I would fain convince you now – that my pursuits and labours, such as they are, are not more selfish than my pleasures, and your future advancement and happiness is the main-spring of them all.

Dickens became engaged to Catherine just as his writing career was poised to take flight. His first volume of *Sketches by Boz* appeared the day after his twenty-fourth birthday in February 1836, and publication of his first novel, *The Pickwick Papers*, began in serial form at the end of March, two days before they married. Had Dickens been famous earlier, or married later, would he have chosen the same life partner?

As the wedding day approached, Catherine was clearly still exercised over the time Dickens spent working. As he explained on 6 March: 'You must not be "coss" with what I cannot help.'

I like the *matter* of what [writing] I have done today but the quantity is not sufficient to justify my coming out tonight. If the representations I have made to you, about my working as a duty, and not as a pleasure to keep you in good humour ... why, then, my dear, you must be out of temper, and there is no help for it!

The wedding was fixed for St Luke's Church, Chelsea on 2 April 1836. The singer Henry Burnett, husband of Dickens's musician sister Fanny, commented:

All things passed off very pleasantly, and all seemed happy, not the least so Dickens and his young girlish wife. She was a bright, pleasant bride, dressed in the simplest and neatest manner.[1]

The wedding was a quiet affair, with only a couple of guests beyond the immediate members of the two families, for 'Mr Dickens had not yet taken hold, as soon after he did, of the busy and talented men', commented another brother-in-law, the architect and civil engineer Henry Austin, husband of Dickens's sister Letitia.

The honeymoon was spent at Chalk, near Gravesend, and by the time the young couple returned to London, Catherine was already pregnant. Over the next sixteen years she would give birth to a total of ten children, all but one of whom survived to adulthood, and she suffered at least two miscarriages.[2]

In later life, Dickens would complain to friends that he had so many children, as if this had nothing to do with him.[3] Even his daughter Katey commented on the fact.[4] Why he assumed no responsibility for this, if he felt so strongly about it, is unclear. Contraceptive devices were neither illegal nor unavailable in Victorian Britain, even though publishing information about available methods was against the law. Contraception was, of course, abhorrent to some on moral and religious grounds, even towards the end of the nineteenth century, by which time it was widely practised among the upper classes. Statesman William Gladstone, for example, deeply deplored what he called 'the American sin' which, together with divorce, he regarded as one of the 'disintegrating causes' affecting standards of conjugal morality.[5] Dickens may have been of the same opinion.

Catherine being of a retiring and nervous disposition, and Dickens being increasingly taken up with his writing, her younger sister Mary Scott Hogarth[6], who had acted as their chaperone during their courting days, joined the Dickens household after their marriage, in order to keep Catherine company and to help with domestic affairs. It was an arrangement made in heaven. Dickens doted on his young sister-in-law, who became 'the dearest friend I ever had'.

On the evening of 6 May 1837, a year after their marriage, Dickens, Catherine and Mary went to the St James's Theatre to see the opening performance of *Is She His Wife? or Something Singular*, a one-act comic burletta for which Dickens had written the script some years before. They returned to the Dickens's new home in Doughty Street,[7] and Mary retired to her bedroom on the top floor some time after one o'clock, 'in perfect health and her usual delightful spirits'. Shortly afterwards, she collapsed. Dickens heard a cry from her room. A doctor was sent for but the case was hopeless: 'Everything that could possibly be done *was* done, but nothing could save her. The medical men imagine it was a disease of the heart.'

At three o'clock the following afternoon, Mary Hogarth died. After her death, Dickens took a ring off her finger and wore it for ever; he took her clothes and hung them in his wardrobe; he took a lock of her hair and kept it in a locket; and he made plans to be buried in the plot next to her at Kensal Green cemetery.

Mary was buried on 13 May. Dickens composed the inscription for her gravestone. It read: 'Young Beautiful And Good/God in His Mercy Numbered Her With His Angels/At The Early Age Of Seventeen'.

Four days later, he wrote to Thomas Beard, his oldest friend from school days, describing how he was deeply 'shaken and unnerved by the loss of one whom I so dearly loved'.

Thank God she died in my arms, and the very last words she whispered were of me. Of our sufferings at the time, and all through the dreary week that ensue, I will say nothing – no one can imagine what they were. You have seen a good deal of her, and can feel for us, and imagine what a blank she has left behind. The first burst of my grief has passed, and I can think and speak of her calmly and dispassionately. I solemnly believe that so perfect a creature never breathed. I knew her inmost heart, and her real worth and value. She had not a fault.

Two weeks later, on 31 May, in a letter to writer Richard Johns, he added that Catherine's sister, 'from the day of our marriage had been the grace and life of our home, our constant companion, and the sharer of all our little pleasures'. He should have known, he wrote, that such happiness could not last.

The change has come, and it has fallen heavily upon us. I have lost the dearest friend I ever had. Words cannot describe the pride I felt in her. And the devoted attachment I bore her. She well deserved it, for with abilities far beyond her years, with every attraction of youth and beauty, and conscious as she must have been of everybody's admiration, she had not a single fault, and was in life almost as far above the foibles and vanity of her sex and age as she is now in Heaven.

Catherine continued to suffer 'most deep and bitter anguish', he added. That same day, he wrote to another friend, Harrison Ainsworth, describing Mary as 'the dear girl whom I loved, after my wife, more deeply and fervently than anyone on earth'.

Dickens continued to be haunted by the image of Mary all his life. During a visit that same year to Yorkshire with his illustrator Hablot Browne ('Phiz') to research conditions in the notorious boarding schools in the north of the county – research which would provide the background to *Nicholas Nickleby* – he wrote to Catherine on 1 February 1838, with little apparent regard of what she might feel about such fervent posthumous devotion to her sister:

Is it not extraordinary that the same dreams which have constantly visited me since poor Mary died, follow me everywhere? After all the change of scene and fatigue, I have dreamt of her ever since I left home, and no doubt shall until I return. I should be very sorry to lose such visions for they are very happy ones – if it be only the seeing her in one's sleep – I would fain believe, too, sometimes, that her spirit may have some influence over them, but their perpetual repetition is extraordinary! Extraordinary indeed!

On 13 October 1841, Mary's grandmother died, and the decision was made to bury her beside Mary, the resting-place that Dickens had hoped would be his. Shortly afterwards, Mary's brother George died and was buried in the same plot. 'It is a great trial to me to give up Mary's grave,' he wrote to Forster on 25 October,

... greater that I could possibly imagine. I thought of moving her to the catacombs, and saying nothing about it; but then I remembered that the poor old lady [Mary's grandmother] is buried next to her at her own desire, and could not find it in my heart, directly she is laid in the earth, to take her grandchild away. The desire to be buried next her is as strong upon me now, as it was five years ago; and I *know* (for I don't think there ever was love like that I bear her) that it will never diminish. I fear I can do nothing. Do you think I can? They would move her on Wednesday, if I resolve to have it done.

'I cannot bear the thought of being excluded from her dust', he added,[8]

and yet I feel that her brothers and sisters, and her mother, have a better right that I hope to be placed beside her. It is but an idea. I neither think nor hope (God forbid) that our spirits would ever mingle *there*. I ought to get the better of it, but it is very hard. I never contemplated this – and coming so suddenly, and after being ill, it disturbs me more than it ought. It seems like losing her a second time.

The following year, 1842, a good five years after Mary's

death, when Dickens was visiting Niagara Falls during his first American reading tour, he still sensed the presence of his late sister-in-law.

On the day after the sixth anniversary of Mary's death, on 8 May 1843, Dickens wrote to his mother-in-law recalling the sad occasion, and how

after she died, I dreamed of her every night for many months – I think for the best part of a year – sometimes as a spirit, sometimes as a living creature, never with any of the bitterness of my real sorrow, but always with a kind of quiet happiness, which became so pleasant to me that I never lay down at night without a hope of the vision coming back in one form or another, And so it did. I went down into Yorkshire, and finding it still present in me, in a strange scene and a strange bed, I could not help mentioning the circumstance in a note I wrote home to [Catherine]. From that moment, I have never dreamed of her once, though she is so much in my thoughts (especially when I am successful, and have prospered in anything) that the recollection of her is an essential part of my being, and is as inseparable from my existence as the beating of my heart is.

Mrs Hogarth's response is not recorded; but she must have been relieved, at least, that Dickens's dreams of one of her daughters (his sister-in-law) ceased once he related them to another of her daughters (his wife).

Mary Hogarth was the model for Rose Maylie, sister of the hero's dead mother in *Oliver Twist*, which Dickens began writing in 1837, the year of Mary's death. Like the real Mary, Rose was 'in the lovely bloom and springtime of womanhood; at the age, when, if ever angels be for God's good purposes enthroned in mortal forms, they may be, without impiety, supposed to abide in such as her'. Rose, like Mary, was just seventeen, slight and 'exquisite'. She was 'mild and gentle ... pure and beautiful ... The very intelligence that shone in her deep blue eyes … the sweetness and good humour … above all, the smile, the cheerful, happy, smile, were made for Home, and fireside peace and happiness.' The advantage that Rose had over Mary was that, being fictional, she could be kept alive.

The tragedy of Mary was also the driving force behind Dickens's description of the death of Little Nell in *The Old Curiosity Shop*. Dickens admitted he had conjured up the memory of the death of Mary to enable him to write Little Nell's death scene. On 8 January 1841, Dickens wrote to Forster that he had nearly completed the sad episode, but it was hard going.

I only began yesterday, and this part of the story is not to be galloped over, I can tell you. I think it will come famously – but I am the wretch-edest of the wretched. It casts the most horrible shadow on me, and it is as much as I can do to keep moving at all. I tremble to approach the place …I shan't recover from it for a long time. Nobody will miss her like I shall. It is such a very painful thing to me, that I really cannot express my sorrow. Old wounds bleed afresh when I only think of the way of doing it: what the actual doing it will be, God knows. I can't preach to myself the schoolmaster's consolation, though I try. Dear Mary died yesterday, when I think of this sad story. I don't know what to say about dining tomorrow – perhaps you'll send up tomorrow morning for news? That'll be the best way. I have refused several invitations for this week and next, determining to go nowhere until I had done. I am afraid of disturbing the state I have been trying to get into, and having to fetch it all back again.

Shortly after Mary's funeral, to help Catherine recover from the shock of her death and her subsequent miscarriage – and to regain his own composure – Dickens took his wife away for a month's convalescence at a farm in Hampstead. By the time they returned to Doughty Street, she was pregnant once again. Their second child, a daughter, was born on 6 March 1838; they called her Mary, in memory of her late aunt. Charles and Catherine

Dickens, aged twenty-six and twenty-three respectively, had not yet been married two years.

They were the parents of four by the time they embarked on their six-month tour of America, in January 1842. Dickens, now nearly thirty, was minded to see the New World as a land of endless promise and opportunity. He persuaded his then publishers, Chapman and Hall, to fund the trip, on the grounds that the publicity it engendered would enhance his profile, and thus the sale of his books back home; and he persuaded his wife Catherine that their four children – Charley, Mamey, Katey and Walter – could safely be left behind under the joint supervision of their Uncle Fred, Dickens's younger brother, and the Dickens's great friends, the actor William Charles Macready (1793–1873) and his wife, Kitty.[9] The Hogarths had also undertaken to help out at Tavistock House, and the Dickenses set sail in January for New York on board the steamer *Britannia*.

During their six-month stay in America, the Dickenses were widely feted, wined and dined, generally celebrated and universally admired. The Valentine's Day 'Boz' ball – so called after Dickens's early pseudonym – was a particular success. They were introduced to two presidents: the retired sixth president, John Quincy Adams (1767–1848) and the current incumbent, John Tyler (1790–1862), the country's tenth head of state. They were also introduced to the great and good of American literary life, including abolitionist and author Harriet Beecher Stowe (about to write *Uncle Tom's Cabin*); poet and translator of Dante, Henry Wadsworth Longfellow; short-story writer and inventor of the detective genre, Edgar Allan Poe; author and physician Oliver Wendell Holmes; and poet James Russell Lowell.

Under circumstances that were sometimes difficult, Catherine proved herself indispensable, acting as Dickens's secretary, personal assistant, and diplomatic buffer between her husband and people with whom he did not want to be bothered. If Dickens felt disinclined to deal with his public, Catherine would step in on his behalf. Americans thought her 'an excellent woman ... natural in her manners, seems not at all elated by her new position, but rests upon a foundation of good sense and good feeling.'[10] In a letter to his friend the artist Daniel Maclise (1807–70), Dickens described the pair of them as acting out 'a kind of Queen and Albert'.

At the beginning, Dickens was entranced with his reception. But as he began to exploit this to some degree to raise the debate on the question of international copyright – one of his hobby-horses, since it deprived writers of much that was due to them – he sensed his campaign being thwarted by vested interests, and felt himself increasingly 'shocked and disturbed by the treatment I have received here ... This is not the Republic I came to see. This is not the Republic of my imagination'. American publishers regarded the work of non-resident authors as unprotected by copyright, and they were widely pirated.[11]

By June 1842, the Dickenses were back in London. The separation had proved difficult for the children – Charley, in particular, was unwell for some time as a result. No children were conceived during the American trip but it was not long before Catherine was pregnant again, and in 1844 their fifth child, Frank, was born.

About this time, Catherine's younger sister Georgina, then just fifteen years old, joined the household as companion and help. With the support of a sister, Catherine's pregnancies and post-natal experiences would never again be as bad as they had been since the death of Mary six or so years earlier.

The image of dear, dead Mary was said by the Hogarths to

be rekindled in the face of a young musician Dickens met on 26 February 1844. He had been invited to chair a soirée at the Liverpool Mechanics' Institution. The musical entertainment for the evening was provided by a young woman called Christiana Weller, who played a fantasia on the piano. Dickens became immediately infatuated by the pretty eighteen-year-old.

The following day, he invited himself to lunch with Christiana's family. He had written 'a bit of doggerel' for her to put in her album. With an allusion to his fictional character Sam Weller in *The Pickwick Papers*, it read:

I put in a book once, by hook or by crook.
The whole race (as I thought) of a 'feller'
Who happily pleas'd the town's taste (much diseas'd)
And the name of this person was Weller.
I find to my cost that *One Weller* I lost.
Cruel Destiny so to arrange it!
I love her dear name which has won me such fame,
But Great Heaven how gladly I'd change it!

The only way a man could change a woman's name was to marry her. However appropriate Dickens may have thought this was for an already married man, he made no secret of his infatuation. The following day, he wrote a letter to his friend Thomas Thompson, describing the evening in Liverpool and confessing how smitten he was with Christiana.

I cannot joke about Miss Weller; for she is too good; and interest in her (spiritual young creature that she is, and destined to an early death I fear) has become a sentiment with me.

Good God, what a mad man I should seem if the incredible feeling I have conceived for that girl could be made plain to anyone!

To the girl's father he wrote, enclosing two volumes of Tennyson's poetry for her and saying that he was unsure whether he should comment, but Christiana's 'great gifts and uncommon character' had 'inspired him with an interest which I should labour in vain to express to you'.

I see many people as you suppose; and many whom Nature has endowed with talents of one kind or another. The figures which come and go before me are so numerous, and change so constantly, that, however bright they may be, I am not accustomed to care much for them, or to feel any great degree of concern in their proceedings. But I read such high and such unusual matter in every look and gesture of the spiritual creature who is naturally the delight of your heart … that she started out at once from the whole crowd the instant I saw her and will remain there always in my sight. Your affection will not be displeased to hear this I know.

Imagine, then, Dickens's surprise when, just two weeks after he met Christiana, he received word from Thompson that he was equally smitten, and was actively courting the girl. The letter made 'the blood go from my face to I don't know where,' Dickens replied, 'and my very lips turned white. I never in my life was so surprised.' He encouraged Thompson to press his suit, as he would have done himself, had he been free.

If I had all your independent means, and twenty times my own reputation and fame, and felt as irresistibly impelled towards her as I should if I were in your place and as you do, I would not hesitate … but would win her if I could, by God! I would answer it to myself, if my world's breath whispered to me that I had known her but a few days, that hours of hers are years in the lives of common women.

But again he repeated his conviction that Christiana was doomed to an early death, partly because her father was allowing her to be excessively taxed by her hectic musical career.

The course to which he is devoting her should not be called her life but Death; for its speedy end is certain. I saw an angel's message in her face that day that smote me to the heart.. He may not know this, always being with her; it is very likely he does not; and I would tell it him. Repose, change, a mind at rest, a foreign climate would be, in a springtime like hers, the dawning of a new existence. I believe … that this would save her. But at the worst contemplating … the distant chance … of what is so dreadful, I could say in solemn and religious earnestness that I could better bear her passing in my arms to Heaven than I could endure the thought of coldly turning off into the World again to see her no more; to have my very name forgotten in her ears.

After some initial resistance from her family, Thompson married Christiana, at which point Dickens lost all interest. Far from being condemned to an early grave, she lived to the ripe old age of eighty-five and had two daughters; one became the poet, essayist and suffragist, Alice Meynell (1846–1933), the other the painter Lady ('Mimi') Butler (1847–1922). Dickens visited the family on one occasion during a visit to Italy, where he was rather waspishly critical of her housekeeping style.

Dickens's fear that the girl was doomed to die young had no basis in reality. Perhaps Mary Hogarth's demise, at about the same age as Christiana was when he met her, had predisposed him to associate idealized innocence, youth and beauty with inevitable death; perhaps he found the death of a young virgin more romantic than a maturing sexuality.

Catherine Dickens must have been unaware of the depth of her husband's infatuation with Christiana Weller in early 1844, since she became close friends with the girl for a short while. (Dickens's brother Frederick went on to marry Christiana's sister, Anna.) But Catherine was painfully conscious of his next obsession, which played out in front of her very eyes a few months later in Italy, which dragged on for years, and which prompted even this long-suffering wife to protest.

Dickens had decided to take the family to the Continent for a year. His latest novel, *Martin Chuzzlewit*, wasn't doing as well as he hoped, and reviews of *American Notes* were disappointing. He was feeling tired and jaded and lacking new ideas, and there were so many demands on his purse within the extended family that it made financial sense to let their London home and rent somewhere in Italy for a year, where they could live much more cheaply. A tenant was found for the house on Devonshire Terrace; Dickens bought a massive second-hand coach for just forty-five pounds; and on 2 July, two days after the final instalment of *Martin Chuzzlewit* was published, the entire Dickens ménage – two parents, five children, Aunt Georgy, two nurses, a courier and the family dog – set off in the coach for Genoa. A villa had been rented on their behalf – the Villa Bagnerello at Albaro – but it was overpriced and overrun with vermin, and after a couple of months they moved to the Palazzo Peschiere in the centre of town.

They had just moved into the palazzo when Dickens had a dream of Mary. 'I was visited by a Spirit,' he wrote to Forster. 'I could not make out the face, nor do I recollect that I desired to do so.'

Anyway, I knew it was poor Mary's spirit. I was not at all afraid, but in a great delight, so that I wept very much, and stretching out my arms to it called it 'Dear' … It was so full of compassion and sorrow for me – which I knew, spiritually, for, as I have said, I didn't perceive its emotions by its face – that it cut me to the heart.

He awoke 'with the tears running down my face', and woke his wife to repeat what he had experienced. But it was not the fact of her husband's being visited, yet again, by the vision of her dead sister that upset Catherine Dickens; rather, it was his increasingly intimate involvement in calling up visions, through hypnosis, in the mind of one of their new friends in Genoa, the de la Rues.

Emile de la Rue was an eminent Swiss banker; he counted among his closest friends the statesman Camillo Cavour, who would become the first prime minister of the new kingdom of Italy. His English-born wife, Augusta (née Granet), was a semi-invalid who suffered from a range of nervous ailments, including generalized anxiety, convulsions, sleep disturbances and a serious facial tic. Dickens had experimented with mesmerism for some time – Catherine and Georgy, among others, had proved susceptible to his hypnotic powers. For whatever reason, Dickens, utterly convinced of his powers of 'animal magnetism', decided he was able to help this 'excellent little woman' (another 'little woman') through mesmerism and, around Christmas 1844, began a course of 'treatment' with her; it lasted for several months intensively, and for a period of years overall, during which time he believed that he was 'struggling for control of her psyche with a sinister evil phantom'.[12] 'I have the truest interest in her and her sufferings,' he wrote to her husband, 'and if I could lessen them in any degree, I should derive great happiness from being the fortunate instrument of relief.' His intense involvement with the case caused Catherine Dickens, understandably, no little distress.

Mesmerism was an early form of hypnotism which took its name from Friedrich Mesmer (1734–1815). German-born, Mesmer settled in Paris in 1778 but fled to London at the time of the French Revolution. Its followers hailed mesmerism as a cure for the world's troubles, a way by which human energy could be directed, or redirected, by the strong will of another.

Dickens's interest in mesmerism was aroused by his family doctor, James Elliotson, who was a staunch advocate and whom, despite career setbacks, Dickens supported until his death. While Dickens seems to have learned the trick of mesmerizing people, practising successfully on both Catherine and Georgy, he appears never to have submitted to being hypnotized himself.

Having established that, during hypnosis, he was apparently able to minimize Augusta de la Rue's tic, calm her anxieties and improve her sleep pattern, Dickens became increasingly interested in delving the deeper recesses of the psyche of Mme de la Rue, who was allegedly also being haunted in her dreams by a nameless ghost.

The 'treatment' continued even at a distance, while the Dickens family were touring Italy. Dickens endeavoured to hypnotize Augusta remotely; but, on one bizarre occasion, the intervention seemed to work on Catherine instead. Dickens found he had cast his wife into a trance, while the experience proved less effective for Augusta, back in Genoa, whose – possibly hysterical – condition became significantly worse while the great novelist was away from her.

The two families met up again in Rome (Dickens arranged this without consulting Catherine) where the 'treatment' resumed on an almost daily basis, at any time of the day or night, as required. Dickens's complete conviction that he was uniquely competent to cure such a malady was breathtaking enough. That he was insensitive enough to indulge his egotism at the expense of the obvious pain caused to Catherine by such intimate involvement with – and emotional control over – another woman is staggering. Dickens's response to Catherine's distress and embarrassment was counter-accusation and denial. To the de la Rues, he belittled his wife's attitude as mindless jealousy to the point of nervous breakdown, even referring to it years later as supporting evidence at the time of the marital separation. To Emile de la Rue, he explained the husband's inability to achieve with his wife what Dickens could achieve as pure bad luck.

Catherine at least felt brave enough in asserting herself to insist that, on their next trip to the Continent the following year, they would not go as far as Genoa, and thus avoid the de la Rues. (But even as late as 1853, when Dickens was touring Italy with Wilkie Collins and Augustus Egg, he still harped back to the subject, writing to Catherine, left behind in England, with a request that she correspond in the warmest terms with Mme de la Rue.)

After their return from a year in Italy in 1845, Dickens had found his second wind. In the decade or so since his marriage to Catherine in 1836, he had given the world *The Pickwick Papers*, *Oliver Twist*, *Nicholas Nickleby*, *The Old Curiosity Shop*, *Barnaby Rudge*, *Martin Chuzzlewit*, and, while they were in Italy, *A Christmas Carol*. The year's break had clearly worked its magic and restored him to his previous form, and 1846 saw the beginning of the publication, in serial form, of *Dombey and Son*. In 1847, he began his collaboration with the philanthropist Angela Burdett-Coutts on the Urania Cottage hostel for fallen women, a project that would claim much of his time until the late 1850s. *David Copperfield* ('my favourite child') was launched in 1850 and instalments of *Bleak House* began to appear in 1851; in 1853, Dickens gave his first public reading of *A Christmas Carol*. Serialized instalments of *Hard Times* first appeared in *Household Words* in 1854. *Little Dorritt* was waiting in the wings.

And then, in 1855, something happened that threw Dickens completely off course.

On the evening of 9 February 1855, two days after his forty-third birthday, Dickens was sitting by the fire at his home in Tavistock House, going through his post with no great enthusiasm. But there was something about the look of one of the letters that left him curiously disturbed. He turned it over again,

and suddenly the remembrance of your hand came upon me with an influence that I cannot express to you. Three or four and twenty years vanished like a dream, and I opened it with the touch of my young friend David Copperfield when he was in love.

The letter was from Maria Beadnell Winter, and Dickens was transfixed.

There was something so busy and so pleasant in your letter – so true and cheerful and frank and affectionate – that I read on with perfect delight until I came to your mention of your two little girls. In the unsettled state of my thoughts, the existence of these dear children appeared such a prodigious phenomenon, that I was inclined to suspect myself of being out of my mind, until it occurred to me, that perhaps I had nine children of my own! Then the three or four and twenty years began to rearrange themselves in a long procession between me and the changeless Past, and I could not help considering what strange stuff all our little stories are made of.

Believe me, you cannot more tenderly remember our old days and our old friends than I do. I hardly ever go into the City but I walk up an odd little court at the back of the Mansion House and come out by the corner of Lombard Street. Hundreds of times as I have passed the church there – on my way to and from the Sea, the Continent, and where not – I invariably associate it with somebody (God knows who) having told me that poor Anne [Maria's sister and wife of his friend Kolle] was buried there … I forget nothing of those times. They are just as still and plain and clear as if I had never been in a crowd since, and had never seen or heard my own name out of my own house. What should I be worth, or what would labour and success be worth, if it were otherwise!

Your letter is more touching to me from its good and gentle associations with the state of Spring in which I was either much more wise or much more foolish than I am now – I never know which to think it

– than I could tell you if I tried for a week. I will not try at all. I heartily respond to it, and shall be charmed to have a long talk with you, and most cordially glad to see you after all this length of time.

Dickens gossiped on about mutual friends – he had bumped into the dreaded Mary Anne Leigh at Broadstairs, he recalled – and about family: 'My mother has a strong objection to being considered in the least old, and usually appears here on Christmas Day in a juvenile cap which takes an immense time in the putting on.' He was going to Paris for a fortnight, he explained, adding how he remembered that 'my existence was once entirely uprooted and my whole Being blighted by the Angel of my soul being sent there to finish her education', but promised to make contact on his return to arrange a meeting.

'I have been much moved by your letter,' he concluded, 'and the pleasure it has given me has some little sorrowful ingredient in it.'

In the strife and struggle of this great world where most of us lose each other so strangely, it is impossible to be spoken to out of the old times without a softened emotion. You so belong to the days when the qualities that have done me most good since were growing in my boyish heart that I cannot end my answer to you lightly. The associations my memory has with you made your letter more – I want a word – invest it with a more immediate address to me that such a letter could have from anybody else. Mr Winter will not mind that. We are all sailing away to the sea, and have a pleasure in thinking of the river we are upon, when it was very narrow and little.

Maria replied almost immediately; just five days after he penned his first letter, Dickens was writing to her from Paris, by return of post, in response to a second one from her. He had enquired whether she wanted anything bringing back from Paris, and she had requested a pair of gloves for one of her daughters, he having once acquired a pair for her. 'I got a heartache when I read your commission,' he wrote,

and yet it is a great pleasure to be entrusted with it, and to have that share of your gentler remembrances which I cannot find it still my privilege to have without a stirring of the old fancies. I need not tell you that it shall be executed to the letter – with as much interest as I once matched a little pair of gloves for you which I recollect were blue ones. (I wonder whether people generally wore blue gloves when I was nineteen or whether it was only you!) … I hope now you know me better you will teach [your little girl], one day, to tell her children, in times to come when they may have some interest in wondering about it, that I loved her mother with the most extraordinary earnestness when I was a boy.

He reminded her that there was never 'such a faithful and devoted poor fellow' as he had been. She, for whom he would have died 'with the greatest alacrity', was the source of all his powers of 'fancy, romance, energy, passion, aspiration and determination', and the reason he began to fight his way out of poverty and obscurity.

This is so fixed in my knowledge that to the hour when I opened your letter last Friday night I have never heard anybody addressed by your name, or spoken of by your name, without a start. The sound of it has always filled me with a kind of pity and respect for the deep truth I had, in my silly hobbledehoyhood, to bestow upon one creature who represented the whole world to me. I have never been so good a man since, as I was when you made me wretchedly happy. I shall never be half so good a fellow any more.

He wondered whether she may have recognized 'touches of your old self' in David Copperfield's adored but doomed wife, Dora.

People used to say to me how pretty that all was, and how fanciful it was, and elevated it was above the foolish loves of very young men and women. But they little thought what reason I had to know it was true and nothing more nor less.

There are things I have locked up in my own breast and that I never thought to bring out any more. But when I find myself writing to you again 'all to yourself', how can I forbear to let as much light in upon them as will show you that they are there still. If the most innocent, the most ardent, and the most disinterested days of my life had you for their Sun – as indeed they had – and if I know that the Dream I lived in did me good, refined my heart, and made me patient and perse-vering, and if the Dream were all of you – as God knows it was – how can I receive a confidence from you, and return it, and make a feint of blotting all this out.

Dickens asked if he might also have from Maria a letter 'all to myself'. It followed him home from Paris a few days later, shortly after his, and, though its contents are lost, it clearly left him deeply moved. He admitted the correspondence to no one. On 22 February, he wrote;

Ah! Though it is so late to read in the old hand what I never read before, I have read it with great emotion, and with the old tenderness softened to a more sorrowful remembrance that I could easily tell you. How it all happened as it did, we shall never know on this side of Time; but if you had ever told me then what you tell me now, I know myself well enough to be thoroughly assured that the simple truth and energy which were in my love would have overcome everything. I remember well that long after I came of age – I say long; well! it seemed long then – I wrote to you for the last time of all, with a dawn upon me of some sensible idea that we were changing into man and woman, saying would you forget our little differences and separations and let us begin again? You answered me very coldly and reproach-fully – and so I went my way.

But nobody can ever know with what a sad heart I resigned you, or after what struggles and what conflict. My entire devotion to you, and the wasted tenderness of these hard years which I have ever since half loved, half dreaded to recall, made so deep an impression of me that I refer to it a habit of repression which now belongs to me, which I know is no part of my original nature, but which makes me chary of showing my affections even to my children, except when they are very young. A few years ago (just before *Copperfield*) I began to write my life, intending the manuscript to be found among my papers when its subject should be concluded.[13] But as I began to approach within sight of that part of it, I lost courage and burnt the rest. I have never blamed you at all but I have believed until now that you never had the stake in that serious game which I had.

All this mist passes away before your earnest words; and when I find myself to have been in your mind at that thoughtful crisis in your life which you so unaffectedly and feelingly describe, I am quite subdued and strangely enlightened.

Dickens explained the fact that he had not been in touch with Maria for so many years on the grounds that he would have found it impossible to set his 'old passion aside, as to talk to you like a person in an ordinary relation towards me'. This, he thought, was the main reason why 'the few opportunities that there have been of our seeing one another again have died out'.

All this again you have changed and set right – at once so courageously, so delicately and gently, that you open the way to a confidence between us which still once more, in perfect innocence and good faith, may be between ourselves alone. All that you propose, I accept with my whole heart. Whom can you trust if it be not your old lover? Lady Olliffe asked me in Paris the other day (we are, in our way, confidential you must know) whether it was really true that I used to love Maria Beadnell so very, very, very much. I told her that there was no woman in the world, and there were very few men, who could imagine how much.

Dickens warned Maria that he was 'a dangerous man to be seen with, for so many people know me'; but he stressed that he should 'very much like to see you before we meet when others are by – I feel it, as it were, so necessary to our being at ease'. He suggested she call at Tavistock House the following Sunday afternoon, at a time when his wife Catherine would almost certainly not be at home. In conclusion, he wrote: 'Remember, I accept all with my whole soul, and reciprocate all'. The scene was set for a major emotional rekindling of what had previously been the love of his life.

In one of her letters to Dickens, Maria had described herself as 'toothless, fat, old and ugly'.

'I don't believe [it],' he responded.

The problem was: it was true. Not only that; according to Georgina, she had become 'quite commonplace'. Dickens was absolutely shattered. Whether or not they met that Sunday or on some other occasion, he was utterly disillusioned when they did, and the relationship on his side quickly slid into a platitudinous exchange of pleasantries into which he enrolled the support of other family members, doubtless for reasons of propriety. In his correspondence, she ceased to be 'My dear Maria' and became, once again, 'My dear Mrs Winter'. The dream had dissolved.

However, the rekindling – however brief – of youthful passion had triggered in Dickens a strange unease. Maria was fat and unattractive. So, to be honest, was his wife. Once again, he had the sense of something eluding him, some happiness lurking just around the corner, out of sight. Maria Beadnell had not quenched the longing; on the contrary, she had stoked the fire. She had reminded him of what it was like to be nineteen again. And the fire would not go out.

As a writer, Dickens was never one to let any life experience go unused. Five or six years earlier, he had immortalized young Maria as the dizzy, adorable but ultimately doomed

Dora, 'child-wife' in *David Copperfield* (1849–50), the tender 'Little Blossom', as his aunt Betsey Trotwood described her. Soon after Maria's reappearance in his life – fair, fat and forty now – Dickens immortalized her again, this time as the silly, middle-aged, overblown blossom Flora Finching in *Little Dorrit* (1855–7). 'I am so glad you like Flora,' he wrote to the Duke of Devonshire on 5 July 1856, adding rather ungallantly: 'It came into my head one day that we have all had our Floras (mine is living and extremely fat).'

The reunion with Maria Beadnell in 1855 had proved a massive disappointment for Dickens. But the reliving of his first great passion, at least in the days before they met face to face, had released a deep longing in him just as he was feeling increasingly restless, dissatisfied with his marriage and weighed down with domestic responsibilities.

Dickens was a middle-aged man, with a stout, placid, middle-aged wife, a raft of financial commitments within the extended family, and a horde of children between the ages of three and eighteen. Walter and Frank, and Alfred and Edward had not yet been dispatched abroad, to India and Australia respectively, nor Sydney to the Navy.[14] All the ingredients were in place for a mid-life crisis. He tried to explain his feelings to his friend Forster in a letter from Paris on 13 April 1856.

However strange it is never to be at rest, and never satisfied, and ever trying after something that is never reached, and to be always laden with plot and plan and care and worry, how clear it is that it must be, and that one is driven by an irresistible might until the journey is worked out!

It was much better to go on and fret, however, 'than to stop and fret'. But he hankered after 'the old days – the old days! Shall I ever, I wonder, get the frame of mind back as it used to be then? I find that the skeleton in my domestic closet is becoming a pretty big one.'

A few days after his letter to Forster, Dickens wrote to Wilkie Collins with news from the French capital. As he often did, he joked, in an apparent teasing manner, about Catherine's clumsiness and the amount she ate and drank, but there was a growing sense of irritation: 'I took Mrs Dickens, Georgina, and Mary and Katey to dine at the Trois Frères,' he wrote. 'Mrs Dickens nearly killed herself, but the others hardly did that justice to the dinner that I had expected.'[15]

Restless, dissatisfied, yearning for something more, and with his natural sense of entitlement, it would not be long before Dickens found it.

It was in the summer of 1857 that Dickens first made the acquaintance of the teenage actress Nelly Ternan and her widowed mother and sisters at a benefit performance in Manchester of *The Frozen Deep*, a play created by himself and Wilkie Collins. Dickens was immediately, totally and irrevocably smitten. He persuaded Collins to accompany him on a walking holiday, the aim of which was to follow the women to Doncaster, where they were performing. On returning to London, he began to take stock of his life. The domestic storm clouds were gathering. On 3 September, he opened his heart to Forster. It was the beginning of a narrative through which he sought to reinvent his marriage as never having been happy. It would have carried more weight had he not already fallen head-over-heels in love with pretty little Nelly Ternan who, as we see in Chapter 5, would change things for ever.

Poor Catherine and I are not made for each other, and there is no help for it. It is not only that she makes me uneasy and unhappy, but that I make her so too – and much more so. She is exactly what you know, in the way of being amiable and complying, but we are strangely ill-assorted for the bond there is between us. God knows she would have been a thousand times happier if she had married another kind of man, and her avoidance of this destiny would have been at least equally good for us both. I am often cut to the heart by thinking what a pity it is, for her own sake, that I ever fell in her way; and if I were sick or disabled tomorrow, I know how sorry she would be. But exactly the same incompatibility would arise, the moment I was well again; and nothing on earth could make her understand me, or suit us to each other. Her temperament will not go with mine. It mattered not so much when we had only ourselves to consider, but reasons have been growing since which make it all but hopeless that we should even try to struggle on. What is now befalling me I have seen steadily coming, ever since the days you remember when Mary was born; and I know too well that you cannot, and no one can, help me. Why I have even written I hardly know; but it is a miserable sort of comfort that you should be clearly aware how matters stand. The mere mention of the fact, without any complaint of blame of any sort, is a relief to my present state of spirits – and I can get this only from you, because I can speak of it to no one else.

Forster wrote back immediately, and Dickens replied, accepting some blame for the marriage breakdown, but exonerating himself to some extent on the basis that it was part of the price one paid for being an artist.

To the most part of what you say – Amen. You are not so tolerant as perhaps you might be of the wayward and unsettled feeling which is part (I suppose) of the tenure on which one holds an imaginative life, and which I have, as you ought to know well, often only kept down by riding over it like a dragoon – but let that go by. I make no maudlin complaint. I agree with you as to the very possible incidents, even not less bearable than mine, that might and must often occur to the married condition when it is entered into when very young. I am always deeply sensible of the wonderful exercise I have of life and its highest sensations, and have said to myself for years, and have honestly and truly felt. This is the drawback to such a career, and is not to be complained of. I say it and feel it now as strongly as ever I did; and as I told you in my last, I do not with that view put all this forward. But the years have not made it easier to bear for either of us; and, for her sake as well as mine, the wish will force itself upon me that something might be done. I know too well it is impossible. There is the fact, and that is all one can say. Nor are you to suppose that I disguise from myself what might be urged on the other side. I claim no immunity from blame. There is plenty of fault on my side, I dare say, in the way of a thousand uncertainties, caprices, and difficulties of disposition; but only one thing will alter all that, and that is, the end which alters everything.

While he continued to lease Tavistock House in London, Dickens had recently bought Gad's Hill Place, near Rochester – a property he had admired since childhood, when his father told him that, if he worked hard enough, he might one day own it. From Gad's Hill he sent a letter to the family servant, Anne Cornelius, at Tavistock House on 11 October 1857, with the apparent anodyne instruction that he wanted 'some little changes made in the arrangement of my dressing-room and bathroom. And as I would rather not have them talked about by comparative strangers, I shall be much obliged to you, my old friend, if you will see them completed before you leave Tavistock House'. It sounded simple enough, but then came the sting: Cornelius was to arrange for the boarding-up of the connecting door between the marital bedroom and the dressing-room, with Dickens in future sleeping in the dressing-room, and Catherine on the other side.

I want the recess of the doorway between the dressing-room and Mrs Dickens's room, fitted with plain white deal shelves, and closed in with a plain light deal door, painted white … The sooner this is done, the better.

There followed explicit instructions as to the choice and

location of furniture in his new bedroom. The first Catherine knew of this was when the door was boarded up.

On 23 October, Dickens wrote a shamefully scurrilous letter to his Genoese banker friend Emile de la Rue, whose wife he had mesmerized endlessly, much to the distress of Catherine, to whom he referred once again – as he had done to Forster – as the 'skeleton' in the family cupboard.

Between ourselves (I beckon Madame de la Rue nearer with my fore-finger, and whisper this with a serio-comic smile), I don't get on better in these later times with a certain poor lady you know if, than I did in those earlier Peschiere days [Genoa, 1844–5]. Much worse. Much worse! Neither do the children, elder or younger. Neither can she get on with herself, or be anything but unhappy. (She has been excruciat-ingly jealous of, and has obtained positive proofs of my being on the most confidential terms with, at least Fifteen Thousand Women of various conditions in life, every condition in life, since we left Genoa. Please respect me for this vast experience.) What we should do, or what the girls would be without Georgy, I cannot imagine. She is the active spirit of the house, and the children dote upon her. Enough of this. We put the Skeleton away in the cupboard, and very few people, comparatively, know of its existence.

Dickens made no secret of his acquaintance with Nelly Ternan, whom Katey described as 'the small, fair-haired, rather pretty actress ... of no special attraction save her youth ... [who] flatters him – he was always appreciative of praise ... He had the world at his feet. She was a young girl of 18, elated and proud to be noticed by him', and eager to be liberated from a precarious existence on the stage, 'a hitherto hard and precarious life'.[16] Early on in the affair, Katey recalled finding her mother dissolved in tears because Dickens had demanded that she call on Nelly, presumably to give some spurious stamp of respectability to their relationship (as he had done with Augusta

Catherine Dickens in later years

de la Rue in Genoa). Katey said she must not. But what Dickens wanted, Dickens got; and Catherine made the call.

The marital crisis finally came to a head when a piece of jewellery ordered by Dickens for Nelly was wrongly delivered to Catherine. Dickens tried to bluff his way out of trouble by pointing out that he often gave trinkets to actresses with whom he had worked.[17] But the tipping-point had been reached; and so began an eight-month nightmare for all concerned.

The Hogarths had been getting on Dickens's nerves for some considerable time, presumably on the not unreasonable grounds that they took Catherine's part in the marital difficulties; even their Scottish accent became loathsome to him. When a separation seemed inevitable, Mrs Hogarth and her daughter Helen initially encouraged Catherine to consider a judicial separation under the new Divorce Act which came into force in 1857 – an Act of which Dickens's own daughter-in-law Anne took advantage in separating from his son, Alfred, who had abandoned her. Before 1857, the legal termination of a marriage was a complicated procedure involving three elements: an ecclesiastical court, a common law court, and a Private Member's Bill in the House of Commons, then to be approved in the House of Lords. Even after the new Act, it was a messy business and Catherine would have had to prove grounds such as would have provoked an enormous scandal; this was not in her nature.[18]

The scandal potential was already daunting enough. By the end of May, Catherine was out of Tavistock House and Dickens was writing to his friends to inform them of the change in his circumstances, and to ensure that he controlled the narrative of the separation. Even as the separation settlement was being negotiated, rumours were circulating – fuelled, Dickens believed, by the Hogarth women – that he had an improper relationship either with his sister-in-law Georgy Hogarth or with a young unnamed actress, or, possibly, with both. Dickens, never the first to blink, refused to negotiate further until he received a formal document clearing him of all impropriety. George Hogarth drew up a document, which Dickens rejected as not going far enough; he drafted his own version, and required that it be signed by Helen and Mrs Hogarth, which they duly did on 29 May. It read:

It having been stated to us that in references to the differences which have resulted in the separation of Mr and Mrs Charles Dickens, certain statements have been circulated that such differences are occasioned by circumstances deeply affecting the moral character of Mr Dickens and compromising the reputation and good name of others, we solemnly declare that we now disbelieve such statements. We know that they are not believed by Mrs Dickens, and we pledge ourselves on all occasions to contradict them, as entirely destitute of foundation.

On 4 June, Catherine signed the separation deed. Hardly was the ink dry on the paper before Dickens published a statement about his domestic affairs, first in *The Times* on 7 June, and then in *Household Words* five days later, thereby ensuring that the whole sorry business was known to a much wider audience than if he had kept his counsel. The statement, headed 'PERSONAL', appeared on the front page of *Household Words*. In the preamble, he stressed how much he cherished his relationship with his reading public; how he had always tried to be honest with them, and to shrug off any 'fabulous stories and unaccountable statements' about himself as 'the shadows insep-arable from the light' of his fame and success. On this occasion, however, he felt compelled to address the rumours surrounding his separation from his wife.

Some domestic troubles of mine, of long-standing, on which I will make no further remark than that it claims to be respected, as being of a sacredly private nature, has lately been brought to an arrangement, which involves no anger or ill-will of any kind ...

By some means, arising out of wickedness, or out of folly ... this trouble has been made the occasion of misrepresentations, most grossly false, most monstrous, and most cruel – involving not only me, but innocent persons dear to my heart, and innocent persons of whom I have no knowledge, if, indeed, they have any existence – and so widely spread, that I doubt if one reader in a thousand will peruse these lines, by whom some touch of the breath of these slanders will not have passed, like an unwholesome air.

Those who know me and my nature, need no assurance under my hand that such calumnies are as irreconcilable with me, as they are, in their frantic incoherence, with each other. But there is a great multitude who know me through my writings, and who do not know me otherwise; and I cannot bear that one of them should be left in doubt, or hazard of doubt, through my poorly shrinking from taking the unusual steps to which I now resort, of circulating the Truth.

I most solemnly declare, then – and this I do, both in my own name and in my wife's name, that all the lately whispered rumours touching the troubles at which I have glanced, are abominably false. And that whosoever repeats one of them after this denial, will lie as wilfully and as foully as it possible for any false witness to lie, before Heaven and earth.

Dickens also tried to have the 'personal statement' published in the magazine *Punch*, whose editor was his friend Mark Lemon, but it was rejected, on the grounds that this was a satirical magazine and the statement wasn't remotely funny. Lemon remained a loyal friend to Catherine after the separation, but Dickens cut him off for ever, as he did the publishers of *Punch*, Bradbury and Evans, forbidding his children – as with the Hogarths – to have any contact with them ever again.

The separation deed settled on Catherine an annual allowance of £600. By mid-July, she was installed in a modern three-storey terraced house on Gloucester Terrace, next to London's Regent Park, and Charley was to live with her. Having reached his majority, he was free to choose what he did, and he chose to live with his mother. Dickens maintained that decision was his, not Charley's.

Under the conditions of the settlement, Dickens agreed to give Catherine free access to her children – not an automatic legal right at the time, when custody of children was invariably granted to fathers. It looked like an enlightened gesture on paper; in reality, Dickens made his children 'fully aware' that he would not be amused by any contact they might have with their mother, or any interest they might show in her welfare.[19]

What was Catherine's portion of blame in the marital breakdown? 'There was nothing wrong with my mother,' Katey Dickens told her friend, Gladys Storey. 'She had her faults, of course, as we all have, but she was a sweet, kind, peace-loving woman, a lady – a lady born.' What faults she had, her daughter conceded, were

principally due to her negativeness and an anxiety in regard to her husband's health, especially concerning his meals which, when he was engrossed in writing, would for hours remain untouched; and the anxiety over the safety of her children.

As a result of her nervousness, Catherine was not consulted over domestic arrangements; indeed, she was actively by-passed.

Between Georgina and John Forster, to facilitate matters for the supposed comfort of Charles, a triangle evolved, in which Mrs Dickens played no part. So that incidents connected with the children and home requiring consideration and adjustment were frequently settled by one or another of these in consultation with the master of the house without any reference to the mistress of it ... who suffered exquisitely under this treatment; this led to many misunderstandings and muddles; and later to the accusation by Miss Hogarth, that she threw the responsibility of her children upon others. An accusation as unkind as it was untrue![20]

Catherine's 'fault', more likely, was that she had failed from the start to keep up with her husband. She was not brilliant or glamorous, witty or flamboyant; she was dull and had grown middle-aged, and Dickens, though middle-aged himself, would not settle for that. He wanted more. So he simply wrote his wife out of the script.

During the separation, Catherine had, by and large, remained aloof from all that was going on – perhaps that long-suffering passivity was one of the things about her that both enraged Dickens and encouraged him to take advantage. She told an aunt that she still loved her husband; but, as the summer progressed, it became clear that she was talking more openly about the Ternan affair. Enraged, Dickens announced that he wanted no more communication with her.

In August, as a final humiliation, he allowed to be made public a document he had written in May, before the final settlement; it was known as the 'violated letter', since Dickens claimed he never intended it to be made public. In it, he cast aspersions on Catherine's alleged mental state, and contrasted her general shortcomings with the virtues of her sister Georgy. Far from wanting to keep the contents of the letter private, he had given it to his readings manager Arthur Smith with 'not only my full permission to show this, but I beg you to show, to anyone who may have been misled into doing me wrong'. In August, presumably having been given the nod by Dickens, Smith passed the letter on to the London correspondent of the *New York Tribune*, where it was published on 16 August, after which it was picked up by the London *Morning Chronicle*, the

Morning Herald and other more scurrilous papers. 'Mrs Dickens and I have lived unhappily together for many years,' Dickens wrote. 'Hardly anyone who has known us intimately can fail to have known that we are, in all respects of character and temperament, wonderfully unsuited to each other,' he claimed, calling on their servant Anne Cornelius as witness that wherever they were, 'in London, in the country, in France, in Italy...', they were 'wonderfully unsuited to each other'. 'Nothing,' he continued, 'has on many occasions stood between us and a separation but Mrs Dickens's sister, Georgina Hogarth.'

From the age of fifteen, she has devoted herself to our home and our children. She has been their playmate, nurse, instructress, friend, protectress, adviser and companion. In the manly consideration which I owe to my wife, I will merely remark of her that the peculiarity of her character has thrown all the children on someone else. I do not know – I cannot by any stretch of fancy imagine – what would have become of them but for this aunt, who has grown up with them, to whom they are devoted, and who has sacrificed the best part of her youth and life to them.

She has remonstrated, reasoned, suffered and toiled, again and again, to prevent a separation between Mrs Dickens and me. Mrs Dickens has often expressed to her sense of affectionate care and devotion in her home – never more strongly than in the last twelve months.

Dickens maintained that, for a long time, Catherine had laboured under 'a mental disorder', that she felt herself 'unfit for the life she had to lead as my wife', and that the two of them had decided to stay together for the sake of the children, but, recently, close friends had persuaded him otherwise. He had, accordingly, made a reasonable settlement on his wife 'as generous as if Mrs Dickens were a lady of distinction, and I ... a man of fortune'. Between him and his children, he added, there was not 'a shadow of doubt or concealment' about the affair. 'All is open and plain among us, as if though we were brothers and sisters. They are perfectly certain that I would not deceive them, and the confidence among us is without a fear.'

Despite the alleged 'violation' by his agent in allowing this document to be published, Dickens and Arthur Smith remained firm friends. Dickens never saw or spoke to Catherine again.

Georgy, praised so highly in the 'violated letter', chose to stay on as Dickens's housekeeper. And why would she not? She had been a member of the household since she was fifteen. She could return to the Hogarths, but they were neither rich nor famous. With Dickens she could enjoy perhaps the most interesting possible life available to a spinster of thirty-one, who would probably not now marry (although she had at least one proposal, from Dickens's friend, the painter Augustus Egg, and possibly another from John Forster). She was lively, witty, competent and reliable; the children loved her. Undepleted by the real business of carrying and bearing children, she had the single woman's energy that Catherine, pregnant or post-natal for most of her married life, could not possibly have mustered. Even Catherine was apparently relieved that she was staying on, knowing that the children would be in good hands. So stay on she did, becoming, for Dickens, 'the best and truest friend man ever had'.

She always insisted that she had tried hard to maintain the relationship between Dickens and her sister. At the same time that Dickens was writing to explain the separation to his friends from his point of view, Georgy, ever the stalwart ally, was doing her bit to support his version of the narrative. At the end of May, before the separation was finalized, she wrote a letter to Maria Beadnell Winter. The subtext may have been that she was justifying her staying on after her sister's departure; indeed it would not have been out of character for Dickens to have prompted her to write it.

I am now going to tell you something which will, I am sure, surprise you, and at the first, shock you. It is that Charles and his wife have agreed to live apart in future.

Believe me when I assure you that I am *perfectly convinced* that this plan will be for the happiness of all. I worked hard to prevent it as long as I saw any possibility, but lately I have come to the conviction that there was no other way out of the domestic misery of this house.

For my sister and Charles have lived unhappily for years – they were totally unsuited to each other in almost every respect – and as the children grew up there was not the usual strong tie between them and her – in short, for many years, although we have put a good face upon it, we have been very miserable at home.

My sister has often expressed a desire to go and live away, but Charles never agreed to it on the girls' account; but lately he thought it must be to their advantage as well as to his own and Catherine's to consent to this and remodel their unhappy home.

So, by *mutual consent* and for the reasons I have told you, *and no other*, they have come to this arrangement.

She is to have a house of her own in London, and her eldest son (at his father's request, and not taking any part or showing any preference in doing it) is to live and take care of her.[21]

The other children remain with their father – his eldest daughter naturally taking her mother's place as mistress of the house. She and Katey and I *work* amongst us, but all the dignity will be Mary's, and she will do the honours modestly, gracefully, and prettily, I know.

Of course, Charles is too public a man to take such a step as this without exciting a more than usual nine-days' wonder – and we have heard of the most wonderful rumours and wicked slanders which have been flying about the town as to the cause of this separation.

To a few of our *real* friends Charles wishes the *truth* to be stated, and they cannot show their friendship better than by quietly silencing with the real solemn truth any foolish or wicked persons who may repeat such lies and slanders.

And so the separation came to pass. 'My father was like a madman when my mother left home,' according to Katey. 'This affair brought out all that was worst – all that was weakest. He did not care a damn what happened to any of us. Nothing could surpass the misery and unhappiness of our home.'[22] This may explain the rate at which Dickens's sons were sent off to distant parts; it certainly explains Katey's unsuitable marriage.

In July 1860, two years after her mother's departure, Katey Dickens married the painter and writer Charles Collins (1828–73), younger brother of her father's friend Wilkie. Although she 'respected him and considered him the kindest and most sweet-tempered of men, [she] was not in the least in love with him';[23] but it was an escape route from her father's unhappy home into the greater freedom she could enjoy as a married woman.

Dickens was not in favour of the match, but he went along with it. However, after the wedding breakfast was over, Mamey found their father in Katey's bedroom,

on his knees with his head buried in Katey's wedding-gown, sobbing … When at last he got up and saw her, he said in a broken voice: 'But for me, Katey would not have left home', and walked out of the room.[24]

CHAPTER 4

Philanthropist

Angela Burdett-Coutts (1814–1906) was the wealthiest woman in Britain after Queen Victoria; possibly, even, the second wealthiest woman in Europe. She was also nineteenth-century Britain's greatest philanthropist. King Edward VII called her 'the most remarkable woman in the kingdom', after his mother, Victoria. For Dickens, she was 'the noblest spirit we can ever know'. She and Dickens first met in 1839.

Dickens had enjoyed the friendship of many influential women from an early age. He was just twenty-four when he began frequenting the salons of the brilliant, beautiful and unconventional Marguerite, Countess of Blessington, where he was introduced to many literati of the time.[1] He became great friends with Lavinia Watson, to whom he dedicated *David Copperfield*, and whose home, Rockingham Castle, was immortalized in *Bleak House* as Chesney Wold. Later, the celebrated American society hostess Annie Fields, wife of Dickens's American publisher and a descendant of President John Adams, became particularly devoted.[2]

Yet none of these relationships was as useful, in terms of social reform, as that which Dickens enjoyed with Miss Coutts.

She was born Angela Burdett, youngest of three daughters of

radical MP Sir Francis Burdett and his wife Sophia. At the age of twenty-three, quite unexpectedly, she inherited half of the assets of the prestigious Coutts Bank on the Strand in London; the bank traced its origins as far back as 1692. She owed her inheritance to the generosity, forbearance and foresight of Harriot Mellon (1777–1837), the second wife of her maternal grandfather Thomas Coutts (1735–1822) who appeared to have been blessed by a very happy first marriage to Angela's grandmother, a former family servant. Mellon, a popular actress before she married Coutts, was much younger than her husband and, on his death in 1822, she inherited his entire estate. Shortly after Thomas Coutts's death she, in turn, married a much younger spouse, the Duke of St Albans (1801–49). However, Mellon had always intended that the Coutts Bank assets should remain within her first husband's banking family and had taken pains to identify which member of the next generation was the most worthy heir. She chose her step-granddaughter, Angela. There were conditions attached: she must take the name Coutts; she must not marry a foreigner (one relative had married a Bonaparte); and she had no right to interfere in the day-to-day operation of the bank. And so it happened.

On receiving her inheritance after her step-grandmother's death in 1837, Miss Coutts moved into her own establishment at 1 Stratton Street, Piccadilly. She took with her as her companion her former governess, Hesther Meredith, who remained with her until her death. When Meredith married doctor William Brown, in 1844, he joined the establishment as Miss Coutts's personal physician.

Dickens first met Miss Coutts at a dinner arranged in mid-1839 by Edward Marjoribanks (1776–1868), a senior partner at Coutts Bank where Dickens was already a valued

Angela Burdett-Coutts

client. The country's richest heiress was a mere twenty-five years old and the century's most acclaimed new writer, already the author of *Pickwick Papers*, *Oliver Twist* and *Nicholas Nickelby*, was just twenty-seven.

The Burdett family had been enthusiastic readers of Dickens's fiction from the very early days. Sir Francis wrote to Angela in 1838, on first reading *Oliver Twist*:

I have finished the first volume of *Oliver Twist*. It is very interesting, very painful, very disgusting, and as the old woman at Edinburgh said, on hearing of the sufferings of Jesus Christ, 'oh dear, I hope it isn't true'. Whether anything like it exists or not, I mean to make enquiries for it is quite dreadful and, to society in this country, quite disgraceful. I will, however, go through it now, though it is anything but entertaining.[3]

Something like it did, indeed, exist, of course. Painful and disgusting it may have been to read, and lacking in entertainment value to Sir Francis. But it had truth, nevertheless, being based to some extent on Dickens's own painful experience of his time at Warren's Blacking Warehouse, and if its 'dreadful' and 'disgraceful' qualities encouraged right-minded people to 'make enquiries' about social ills, then Dickens the social reformer would have been delighted to have achieved so much more than mere entertainment.

Dickens and Miss Coutts established a suitably formal early rapport which softened with time so that, by December of 1839, he was already describing himself as being 'on terms of intimacy with Miss Coutts'. The two exchanged family news and gossip about the latest showbusiness celebrities; they swapped books and he sent her advance copies of work of his that was about to be published; she offered him the use of her box at Drury Lane and Covent Garden. Miss Coutts was captivated.

From the first Angela was enchanted by Dickens. In the first glow of his sudden fame he was remarkably attractive. From his luxuriant hair, lustrous eyes and fresh glowing complexion to the brilliant buckles of his shoes there was such a shine about him. There was also a frankness of expression, a look of goodness that Miss Coutts, like other ladies of the day, found irresistible. If there was a little too much of the dandy in his dress, she could forgive him. She had, after all, seen Disraeli in full bloom.[4]

During 1840–1, the relationship between Dickens and Miss Coutts was consolidated. While he was away on his first American tour, he wrote to her regularly with reports of the parties, the crowds, the excitement of it all. Theirs was not the only Dickens-Coutts correspondence at the time. In his absence, his father John, broke and importunate as ever, approached Coutts Bank for an 'advance' of twenty-five pounds which he implied his son would have sanctioned had he not been so busy before his departure. The bank gave John Dickens short shrift.[5]

On his return from America, Dickens brought back a rocking chair for Miss Coutts and an eagle's feather for her companion. The relationship went from strength to strength. It was to Miss Coutts that Dickens dedicated the first one-volume book of *Martin Chuzzlewit*, and, within just a couple of years of their first acquaintance, Dickens became an indefatigable volunteer on behalf of Miss Coutts's good works. This was no mean feat, acting as unpaid private charity secretary in the service of the woman who was the greatest female philanthropist of the nineteenth century, spending over the course of her lifetime some three million pounds on the welfare and improvement of those less fortunate than herself. And it was all well documented; over 500 letters from Dickens to Coutts survive, one of the largest of Dickens's correspondences.

From then until the break-up of his marriage in 1858, Dickens worked indefatigably on behalf of Miss Coutt's charitable projects, guiding her towards socially useful initiatives. They included the Ragged Schools for the free education of destitute children – indeed, education of the poor, generally; urban sanitation; affordable housing for the disadvantaged of society; and vocational training schools for girls. In exchange for this unpaid help, Miss Coutts acted as unofficial godmother to Dickens's eldest son, Charley, paying for his education at Eton, his two years' apprenticeship in Germany, where he learned the banking trade, and never forgetting to send him a spectacular cake on his birthday, wherever he was, at home or abroad. Dickens provided regular progress reports about Charley, but it was not always good news. The problem, Dickens felt, was that Charley was like his mother. He was gentle and affectionate, Dickens wrote to Miss Coutts shortly after Charley's seventeenth birthday, and 'his inclinations are all good',

but I think he has less fixed purpose and energy than I could have supposed possible in my son. He is not aspiring, or imaginative in his own behalf. With all the tenderer and better qualities which he inherits from his mother, he inherits an indescribable lassitude of character – a very serious thing in a man.

Despite her immense wealth and extreme generosity as a society hostess, Miss Coutts was said to be reserved by nature; in fact, extremely shy. She was not too shy, however, to flout the social conventions of the time and propose marriage to the Duke of Wellington (1769–1852) in 1844, when he was seventy-six and she was thirty. Both her parents had died within a few days of each other in January of that year and she turned to him for solace. Gently, he turned her down, on the grounds that he was too old and cranky, warning her of the 'dismal consequences' to her, were he to take up her offer, and adding that his last days would be 'embittered by the reflection that your life was uncomfortable and hopeless' if she were to 'throw yourself away on a man old enough to be your grandfather'.[6] But they became even closer after the proposal and remained the dearest of friends until his death. Perhaps Miss Coutts and Wellington married secretly after all, in the end; perhaps they did not. What is certain is that, on his death in 1852, his family treated her with all the respect due to a widow.

Wellington exercised considerable influence over her choice of charitable projects, his preference being for church-based initiatives, while Dickens's preference was for socially based projects. Wellington had little sympathy for her desire to establish a hostel where former prostitutes could be redeemed for a more useful life. Statistics showed, Wellington said, 'that there is but little if any hope of saving in this world that particular class of Unfortunates to whom you have referred ... those who earn their Bread by the commission of the Offence.'[7] Yet for Dickens, of all the initiatives on which he worked with Miss Coutts, none was more important for him than what came to be known as the Urania Cottage project for 'fallen women' – a home where, after a year's training, destitute girls would learn the skills necessary to make them good domestic servants at least, and, at best, suitable wives for good men in the colonies. The house opened in November 1847 and operated for fifteen years.[8]

While the range of destitute women taken in to Urania Cottage broadened over the years to include single mothers, out-of-work seamstresses, orphaned daughters of impoverished clergymen and other worthy cases, most of its 'fallen women' in the early years were involved, one way or another, with prostitution.

Prostitution was a massive problem in Victorian Britain, and particularly in its capital city. Estimates as to the number of prostitutes operating in central London in the mid-nineteenth century vary widely, from the probably understated figure of 8,000 suggested by contemporary police reports, to a sensationalized figure of 120,000 that appeared in the press. The campaigning journalist Henry Mayhew, who chronicled the condition of the capital's underclass in the mid-century in his *London Labour and the London Poor*, inclined to a figure of around 80,000, while warning that this was probably a conservative estimate. At the time, the population of London was around two and a half million.[9] It is small wonder that nineteenth-century visitors to the city from abroad, where these things were often much better managed, expressed dismay and amazement at the scale and uncontrolled nature of London prostitution.

The difference in estimates may depend partly on how the term prostitute was defined. Mayhew used three categories. 'Professional Prostitutes' included 'Kept Mistresses' and 'Prima Donnas', described as 'women who are kept by men of independent means ... This is the nearest approximation to the holy state of matrimony, and finds numerous defenders and supporters'. 'Clandestine Prostitutes' included 'Maid Servants' and 'Ladies of Intrigue'. 'Cohabitant Prostitutes' was a wide-ranging group that embraced conscientious objectors to marriage, those who could not afford marriage fees, and those who declined to marry because by doing so they would forfeit an income, for example, officers' widows in receipt of a pension, and those who held property only while unmarried.[10] By comparison, a Metropolitan Police survey of May 1857 categorised prostitutes as belonging to one of three differently defined groups: 'well-dressed, living in brothels', 'well-dressed, walking the streets' or 'low prostitute'.

In a breakdown of the types of employment claimed by 'disorderly' prostitutes taken into custody between 1850 and 1860, police records show that milliner was the most frequent trade given (reflecting, at the very least, that everyone at the time wore hats). Laundresses, shoemakers and tailors formed the next biggest groups. Mayhew queried whether these occupations lent themselves particularly to 'demoralisation' – by which he meant a tendency to moral laxity – and concluded that probably this employment profile simply reflected the absolute numbers working in those particular trades.

Again, an 1858 police survey indicates that most prostitution was concentrated in Stepney, followed by Whitechapel, Lambeth and Southwark. In 1850, the fifth most active district had been Westminster, but by the time of the 1858 survey the business there had dropped by one-third.

The vulnerability of particular trades to economic fluctuations was a key factor in determining the pattern of urban deprivation throughout the nineteenth century. Whether it was the end of the 'Season' in London society that tipped dressmakers and milliners into poverty, or the cotton famines that deprived the Lancashire mill workers of their livelihood, the result was often the same. Some Victorian commentators, such as William Acton, who dedicated his medical career to the cause of state regulation of prostitution, looked for its origins in feminine weakness and the 'overgenerosity' of the female spirit, but the reality was that hard economic times meant that, for many women, prostitution was often the only way to make ends meet. Many Victorian sex workers were only transient fallen women, moving in and out of the profession as family finances dictated. Sometimes, if they were lucky, they might move away from it for ever through an upwardly mobile marriage to a grateful client.

Before the 1834 Poor Law Amendment Act, a modicum of relief was available to the poor through the provision of Outdoor Relief, a parish-based support system that enabled applicants to remain in their own homes, doing what they could to earn a living, but receiving supplementary benefits as well. The new Act introduced by Melbourne's Whig government, overturned those provisions, establishing a workhouse regime so dire that only the most destitute were willing to have recourse to it. Dickens felt so strongly, he wrote *Oliver Twist* in protest. In the workhouse, wives were separated from husbands and children from parents, under conditions so dreadful that they could make even prostitution seem a lesser fate than death, so long as it kept the family together. The plight of the urban poor was further complicated by the new Act's stipulation that, where parish relief remained available, it was to be confined to the parish from which applicants originated, not where they had settled. This effectively meant that migrants from country to town often could make no claim for relief from their new parish; indeed they risked being removed to a parish which they, or even their parents, had left many years before. It also inhibited mobility of labour, since those with a potential claim on their home parish would be reluctant to leave it in search of better employment prospects elsewhere. It was not until 1845, when Peel's Conservative government introduced the Poor Removal Act, that they had any protection. This legislation ensured entitlement to irremovability after five years' continuous residence in a parish, a period reduced to three years by a subsequent Act in 1861.[11]

There were two distinct aspects to prostitute rescue work in Victorian England. Many philanthropically minded people served on committees and helped raised funds for charitable initiatives. Others, such as Dickens and his contemporary, politician and four-time prime minister William Gladstone,[12] wanted to be out on the street, making an immediate and personal difference.

The problem of prostitution in the capital was obvious to anyone who walked the streets of mid-nineteenth century London, day or night (as was its companion evil, the open sale of pornography). Indeed, young men coming up to town could buy a readily available printed guide to such sources of entertainment. But while prostitution was rife, talking about it as a social issue was not. It was rarely discussed publicly, nor would it be for many years. As late as 1869, a campaigning journalist and 'social investigator', James Greenwood, felt himself obliged, in *The Seven Curses of London*, to begin a report on prostitution with an apology to 'the supersensitive reader, who will doubtless experience a shock of alarm at discovering this part's heading'. But he explained that it would be pointless to discuss the 'curses of London' without including prostitution.

Doubtless it is a curse, the mere mention of which, let alone its investigation, the delicate-minded naturally shrinks from. But it is a matter for congratulation, perhaps, that we are not all so delicate-minded. Cowardice is not infrequently mistaken for daintiness of nature. It is so with the subject in question. It is not a pleasant subject – very far from it; but that it is not a sufficient excuse for letting it alone … The monstrous evil in question has grown to its present dimensions chiefly because we have silently borne with it.[13]

London was not particularly well provided with refuges to which prostitutes who wanted to give up the profession could

turn for help. Before the early 1800s, there was just one institution in the capital that had as its aim the rescue of fallen
women. This was the Magdalen Hospital, founded in 1758.
The hospital took in nearly nine thousand women in its first
one hundred years, of whom about two-thirds were 'restored
to friends or relations'.[14] By the middle of the nineteenth
century there were about fifty metropolitan institutions for
the 'reception of the destitute and criminal, or those who are
exposed to temptation' and together they could provide accommodation for about four thousand people at any one time. Most
were supported entirely by voluntary contributions and by
the earnings of the inmates, who were either admitted free of
charge or by payment of a small sum towards their maintenance
costs.[15] This was around five pounds – a sum frequently paid out
to the institutions by people such as Gladstone on behalf of the
women he tried to place with them.

Of the fifty London reformatories noted by Mayhew, twenty-
one were devoted exclusively to 'the rescue and reformation of
fallen women, or such as have been led astray from the path of
virtue'.[16] Ten of the institutions were connected to the Church of
England, while in the remaining eleven the religious instruction
was 'unsectarian and evangelical'. But even here, class prevailed.
Three houses were designed for the 'better educated and higher
class of fallen women', while one provided 'shelter exclusively
to those who have recently been led astray, and whose previous
good character will bear the strictest investigation'.[17] Another
was for girls aged fifteen or younger.

The Urania Cottage project for fallen women, as conceived by
Dickens and Miss Coutts, was something different. Its aim was
to take vulnerable young women and give them the chance to
make something better of their lives. They would most likely be

prostitutes; but they might also be disturbed girls from ill-run workhouses, poor girls from Ragged Schools, the destitute, the seduced and attempted suicides. They might be referred to the home by the police, the courts, the prisons, or other institutions; and, indeed, young women could apply personally.

It was on 26 May 1846 that the first mention of the project that would become Urania Cottage appeared in a letter from Dickens to Miss Coutts. It was clear that he hoped the initiative would receive support from the government as regarded the assisted passage of redeemed women to 'other shores'.

In reference to the asylum, it seems to me very expedient that you should know, if possible, whether the Government would assist you to the extent of informing you from time to time into what distant parts of the World, women could be sent for marriage, with the greatest hope for their future families, and with the greatest service to the existing male population, whether expatriated from England or born there. If these poor women *could* be sent abroad with the distinct recognition and aid of the Government, it would be a service to the effort.

He did not think there would be any problem finding suitable accommodation, there being many houses in and around London that could be adapted as a hostel. It would, of course, be necessary to limit the number of inmates,

but I would make the reception of them as easy as possible … I would put it in the power of any Governor of a London Prison to send an unhappy creature of this kind (by her own choice of course) straight from his prison, when her time expired, to the asylum. I would put it in the power of any penitent creature to knock at the door, and say For God's sake, take me in.

It would be made clear to any woman or girl coming to the asylum, Dickens explained to Miss Coutts, that 'she has come there for *useful* repentance and reform, and because her past way of life has been dreadful in its nature and consequences, and full of affliction, misery and despair *to herself*.

Society has used her ill and turned away from her, and she cannot be expected to take much heed of its rights or wrongs. It is destructive to *herself*, and there is no hope in it, or in her, as long as she pursues it. It is explained to her that she is degraded and fallen, but not lost, having this shelter; and that the means of return to Happiness are now about to be put in her own hands, and trusted to her own keeping.

Should Miss Coutts decide to go ahead with the project, Dickens added:

I do not know whether you would be disposed to entrust me with any share in the supervision and direction of the Institution. But I need not say that I should enter on such a task with my whole heart and soul; and that in this respect, as in all others, I have but one sincere and zealous wish to assist you, by any humble means in my power, in carrying out your benevolent intentions.

The discipline system at the planned hostel would be based loosely on the points system developed by Scottish-born naval officer and penal reformer Alexander Maconochie (1787–1860). In the early 1830s, he was private secretary to Sir John Franklin, Lieutenant-General of the convict settlement at Hobart in Van Diemen's Land (now Tasmania).[18] Maconochie was a deeply religious man, generous, compassionate and committed to the notion of the dignity of man, whatever crime any individual person may have committed.

After Hobart, he was sent as commandant of the penal settlement at Norfolk Island, a small island in the Pacific Ocean between Australia, New Zealand and New Caledonia. There he was able to put his principles into practice through a 'marks' scheme that rewarded and encouraged good behaviour and respected the convicts' basic human dignity. He was not able to have their sentences commuted, but claimed a much lower re-offending rate among his prisoners on release than under other regimes. In 1838, he wrote a book outlining his system, entitled *Thoughts on Convict Management*, which was published in Hobart. In 1846, about the time that Dickens and Miss Coutts were launching the Urania Cottage project, his book *Secondary Punishment – the Marks System* was published in London. It echoes many of the principles of the reward system advocated by the great British prison reformer Elizabeth Fry (1785–1840) two decades earlier in her *Observations on the Visiting, Superintendence and Government of Female Prisoners*, a system that Dickens would have seen in operation when visiting Newgate prison.[19] In 1849, Maconochie was appointed governor of the new prison at Birmingham.[20]

Under the variation of his 'marks' system that Dickens appropriated – a model of startling complexity – the inmates of Urania Cottage were given points under nine headings: truthfulness, industry, temper, propriety of conduct and conversation, temperance, order, punctuality, economy and cleanliness. What the women would be taught at the hostel 'would be grounded in religion, most unquestionably', Dickens wrote. More practically, they would be introduced to a system of training 'which, while it is steady and firm, is cheerful and hopeful'. They would learn 'order, punctuality, cleanliness, the whole routine of household duties – as washing, mending, cooking'.

Dickens envisaged starting with 'some comparatively small number – say thirty', he told Miss Coutts on 26 May 1846,

and I would have it impressed on them, from day to day, that the success of the experiment rested with them, and that on their conduct depended the rescue and salvation of hundred and thousands of women yet unborn. In what proportion this experiment would be successful, it is very difficult to predict; but I think that if the Establishment were founded on a well-considered system, and were well managed, one half of the Inmates would be reclaimed from the very beginning, and after a time the proportion would be much larger.

By May of 1847, Dickens had located a suitable property in Shepherd's Bush, for which the rent was sixty guineas a year. It was

retired, but cheerful. There is a garden, and a little lawn. The taxes are very low. A stable would have to be changed into a wash-house, and I would decidedly fence the garden all round [but] I am sure the house would please you.

It did. Miss Coutts was agreeable, the necessary refurbishment was carried out, and Urania Cottage opened for business in November of that year.

At the time the project was getting under way, Dickens's domestic life was increasingly fraught. A seventh child, Sydney, was born in April 1847; in December, Catherine Dickens became seriously ill after suffering a miscarriage on the train from Edinburgh to Glasgow. By April 1848 she was pregnant again. In September, Dickens's beloved sister Fanny died of tuberculosis. In January 1849, another son was born. Dickens wrote to a woman friend that he had no energy whatsoever for his everyday life: 'I am miserable, I loathe domestic hearts. I yearn to be a vagabond.' But despite everything, Dickens's commitment to the Urania Cottage project never faltered.

Dickens's big vision for the fallen women was that 'these unfortunate creatures are to be *tempted* to virtue. They cannot be dragged, driven or frightened. The sacred duty of everyone involved with Urania Cottage should be first to consider how best to get them there, and then how best to keep them there.'

To coincide with the launch of Urania Cottage, Dickens distributed a leaflet to all fallen women who might benefit from spending time at Urania Cottage. Gladstone was so impressed that he used it himself during much of his forty-year campaign to rescue prostitutes. 'You will see, on beginning to read this letter,' Dickens wrote, 'that it is not addressed to you by name.'

But I address it to a woman – a very young woman still – who was born to be happy and has lived miserably; who has no prospect before her but sorrow, or behind her but a wasted youth; who, if she has ever been a mother, has felt shame instead of pride in her own unhappy child.

You are such a person, or this letter would not be put into your hands. If you have ever wished (I know you must have done so for some time) for a chance of rising out of your sad life, and having friends, a quiet home, means of being useful to yourself and others, peace of mind, self-respect, everything you have lost, pray read it attentively and reflect upon it afterwards,

I am going to offer you, not the chance but the *certainty* of all these blessings, if you will exert yourself to deserve them. And do not think that I write to you as if I felt myself very much above you, or wished to hurt your feelings by reminding you of the situation in which you are placed. God forbid! I mean nothing but kindness to you, and I write as if you were my sister.

Think for a moment what your present situation is. Think how impossible it is that it can ever be better if you continue to live as you have lived, and how certain it is that it must be worse. You know what the streets are; you know how cruel the companions that you find there are; you know the vices practised there, and to what wretched consequences they bring you, even while you are young. Shunned by decent people, marked out from all other kinds of women as you walk along, avoided by the very children, hunted by the police, imprisoned, and only set free to be imprisoned over and over again – reading this very letter in a common jail you have already dismal experience of the truth.

But to grown old in such a way of life, and among such company

– to escape an early death from a terrible disease, or your own maddened hand, and arrive at old age in such a course – will be an aggravation of every misery that you know now, which words cannot describe. Imagine for yourself the bed on which you, then an object terrible to look at, will lie down to die. Imagine all the long, long years of shame, want, crime, and ruin that will arise before you. And by that dreadful day, and by the judgment that will follow it, and by the recollection that are certain to have then, when it is too late, of the offer that is made to you know, when it is NOT too late, I implore you to think of it and weigh it well.

There is a lady in this town [Miss Coutts] who from the windows of her house [in Piccadilly] has seen such as you going past at night, and has felt her heart bleed at the sight. She is what is called a great lady, but she has looked after you with compassion as being of her own sex and nature, and the thought of such fallen women has troubled her in her bed.

She has resolved to open at her own expense a place of refuge near London for a small number of females, who without such help are lost for ever, and to make a HOME for them. In this home they will be taught all household work that would be useful to them in a home of their own and enable them to make it comfortable and happy. In this home, which stands in a pleasant country lane, and where each may have her little flower-garden if she pleases, they will be treated with great kindness: will lead an active, cheerful, healthy life: will learn many things it is profitable and good to know, and being entirely removed from all who have any knowledge of their past career will begin life afresh and be able to win a good name and character.

And because it is this lady's wish that these young women should not be shut out from the world after they have repented and learned to do their duty there, and because it is her wish and object that they may be restored to society – a comfort to themselves and it – they will be supplied with every means, when some time shall have elapsed and their conduct shall have fully proved their earnestness and reformation, to go abroad, where in a distant country they may become the faithful wives of honest men, and live and die in peace.

I have been told that those who see you daily in this place believe that there are virtuous inclinations lingering with you, and that you may be reclaimed. I offer the Home I have described in these few words, to you.

In referring to a 'distant country', Dickens did, of course, mean primarily Australia, where, it was hoped, if Urania Cottage girls did not become 'faithful wives of honest men', they would at least have the skills necessary to secure them a position in domestic service.[21]

By the mid-nineteenth century, Australia had ceased to be simply a prison colony. Transportation of convicts from Britain and Ireland, which began in 1787, finally came to an end in 1868, during which time over 162,000 people had been transported.[22] It ended for a number of reasons. The cost of transportation became excessive, particularly when the government realised that convicts could be gainfully used as forced labour at home. There was also an extensive new prison-building programme in the country, beginning with the construction of London's Pentonville in 1842; this extended the possibility of custodial sentences which the Penal Servitude Act of 1853 offered as an alternative to transportation. Furthermore, the discovery of gold in New South Wales that same year increased the supply of voluntary settlers – indeed some prisoners about that time were outraged to discover that they would not, after all, be transported free of charge to the land of promise.[23]

David Copperfield, written between 1850–1, reflects these three different strands. Uriah Heep is transported, having been found guilty of fraud; the Micawbers, always waiting for something to turn up, go to find fame and fortune, and succeed; while Little Em'ly, seduced, abandoned and 'fallen', goes to Australia with Uncle Peggotty to find redemption and a good marriage. In *Great Expectations*, Abel Magwitch, father of Estella and sponsor of Pip, makes a great fortune in Australia before returning illicitly to England.

In fact, two of Dickens's own sons emigrated to New South Wales to seek their fortune – Alfred, aged nineteen, in 1864 and Edward, aged sixteen, in 1868. The year before Alfred's departure, Frederick, a son of the novelist Anthony Trollope (brother-in-law of Nelly Ternan), had also emigrated to Australia, which may have had some influence.[24]

Dickens was closely involved with every aspect of the management of Urania Cottage and its inmates, consulting his benefactress in the greatest detail at every stage, writing to her sometimes on several occasions in one week. He personally interviewed the applicants referred to the home. If they were found acceptable, he recorded their life histories, after which they were forbidden to talk about their past – and the staff were forbidden to ask, on pain of dismissal.[25]

Dickens was also responsible for recruiting the staff for Urania Cottage, which was something of a mixed blessing. In Georgina Morson (d. 1880), however, he and Miss Coutts found an absolute star.

Georgina Collins was born in Merton Abbey, Surrey. On her marriage to Doctor James Morson she followed him to Brazil, where he was Chief Medical Officer for the Brazilian National Mining Association. They were based at the small town of Cayuba in Matto Grosso, deep in the Brazilian rain forest. James Morson died in 1844, leaving his widow with two small daughters and a third child on the way. Travelling hundreds of miles by mule before talking her way on board a British man-of-war, Georgina Morson made her way to England. Back home, she discovered that her brother-in-law had embezzled what funds she thought her late husband had left her. She also discovered that her late husband had treated Miss Coutts's father many years before, and, having settled her three young children with their grandparents, she applied to Miss Coutts for support. So it was that she fetched up as matron of Urania Cottage, a post she held with great success from 1849 until her remarriage in 1854. From the start, Dickens found Georgina Morson 'very promising' and he was not disappointed. She brought calm and common sense to the project and was sadly missed when she left to marry a bookseller from Sevenoaks.

Among his other duties, Dickens conducted all corre-spondence on behalf of Urania Cottage, paid the bills, kept meticulous accounts, drew up a programme of prayers and installed a small library. For a while, until Miss Coutts called a halt, he even arranged for the women to be given singing lessons by a musician friend who had been a fellow student of his sister Fanny at the Royal Academy of Music. He persuaded William Brown, husband of Miss Coutts's companion Hannah, to act as consultant physician, and a chaplain from Coldbath Fields prison to provide religious instruction. He chose the furnishings, supervised building work and drainage repairs. He even had new drying apparatus designed for the laundry – it would also be used to heat the baths – which was so successful that it was later modified for use in the British military hospitals at Scutari during the Crimean War.[26]

Despite advice to the contrary from his friend George Chesterton, governor of Coldbath Fields prison, Dickens – he of the flamboyant waistcoats – was particularly concerned that the women's clothing should not be dull and institutional. Smart, colourful clothes would cheer them up, he argued to Miss Coutts, and help them maintain a pride in their appearance;

this, in turn, would be important when it came to finding husbands in the colonies.

I constantly notice a love of colour and brightness to be a portion of a generous and fine nature. I feel sure that it is often an innocent part of a capacity for enjoyment, and appreciation, and general adornment of everything, which makes a buoyant genial character. I say most gravely that I do *not* know what it may take away from the good influences of a poor man's home if I strike this natural common thing out of the girl's heart who is to be his wife.

It is like the use of strong drink … the evil is in the abuse, not the use … The natural tendency of the sex, through all its grades, is to a little finery – and I would not rule counter to that … agreeable, wholesome and useful characteristic.

Dickens insisted that the regime at Urania Cottage should not be repressive.

I would have it understood by all – I would have it written up in every room – that they were not going through a monotonous round of occupation and self-denial which began and ended there, but which began, or was resumed, under that roof, and would end, by God's blessing, in happy homes of their own.

After Dickens's estrangement from his wife, he and Miss Coutts also began gently to drift apart. Dr Brown, the husband of her companion, Hannah, had died unexpectedly towards the end of 1855,²⁷ and the two women were spending more time away from London, particularly at a house they had rented in Torquay. Both Miss Coutts and Mrs Brown were aware of the growing tensions in the Dickens's marriage.

In June 1857, Miss Coutts and her companion spent a couple of days at Gad's Hill, Dicken's home in Rochester; also staying there was the Danish writer of fairy tales, Hans Christian Andersen, who found this modern-day banking princess, despite her great wealth, 'a straightforward, kind and good-natured lady'.[28] On their departure, Mrs Brown, fearing Dickens was close to a breakdown, wrote to him, sympathizing over the increasingly fraught state in which he found himself. He was, he wrote back, confirming that he was 'exactly in the state you describe. It belongs to such a life as mine and is its penalty. Thank God while I have health and activity it does not last long, so after a miserable day or two, I have come out of the dark corner into the sun again.'

But the darkness kept returning. In February 1858, Dickens was 'inexpressibly vexed' that Catherine had approached Miss Coutts behind his back to ask for help in finding a job for her youngest brother Edward. The tension was becoming intolerable and, on 9 May 1858, Dickens wrote to Miss Coutts to explain the situation.

You have been too near and too dear a friend to me for many years, and I am bound to you by too many ties of grateful and affectionate regard to admit of my any longer keeping silence to you on a sad domestic topic. I believe you are not quite unprepared for what I am going to say, and will, in the main, have anticipated it.

I believe my marriage has been for years and years as miserable a one as ever was made. I believe that no two people were ever created, with such an impossibility of interest, sympathy, confidence, sentiment, tender union of any kind between them, as there is between my wife and me. It is an immense misfortune to me – it is an immense misfortune to her – but Nature has put an insurmountable barrier between us, which never in this world can be thrown down.

You know me too well to suppose that I have the faintest thought of influencing you on either side. I merely mention a fact which may induce you to pity us both, when I tell you that she is the only person I have ever known with whom I could not get on somehow or other, and in communicating with whom I could not find some way to come to some kind of interest. You know that I have the many impulsive faults which often belong to my impulsive way of life and exercise of fancy; but I am very patient and considerate at heart, and would have beaten out a path to a better journey's end than we have come to, if I could.

We have been virtually separated for a long time. We must put a wider space between us now, than can be found in one house. If the children loved her, or ever had loved her, this severance would have been a far easier thing than it is. But she has never attached one of them to herself, never played with them in their infancy, never attracted their confidence as they grew older, and never presented herself before them in the aspect of a mother. I have seen them fall of from her in a natural – not *un*natural progress of strangement, and at this moment I believe that Mary and Katey (whose dispositions are of the gentlest and most affectionate conceivable) harden into stone figures of girls when they can be got to go near her, and have their hearts shut up in her presence as if they were closed by some horrid spring.

No one can understand this but Georgina, who has seen it grow from year to year, and who is the best, most unselfish, and most devoted of human Creatures …

It is a relief to me have written this to you. Don't think the worse of me; don't think the worse of her. I am firmly persuaded that it is not within the Compass of her Character and faculties to be other than she is. If she had married another sort of man she might however have done better. I think she has always felt herself to be at the disadvantage of groping blindly about me, and never touching me, and so has fallen into the most miserable weaknesses and jealousies. Her mind has, at times, been certainly confused besides.

All this would have sounded much more convincing, had Dickens not already met Nelly Ternan.

Dickens was right: Miss Coutts did not take sides. On receiving her friend's letter describing the rift, she replied, apparently at Catherine's suggestion, urging reconciliation of some sort, but to no avail. 'How far I value your friendship, and how I love and honour you … you can never know,' he wrote on 19 May. 'But nothing on earth, not even you – no consideration, human or Divine, can move me from the resolution I have taken.'

Miss Coutts's intervention had failed; but Catherine, who saw much more of Miss Coutts after the separation than she ever had done before it, was grateful, nevertheless, and wrote to her with thanks 'for your kindness in doing what I asked. I have now – God help me – only one course to pursue. One day ... I may be able to tell you how hardly I have been used'.

In April 1860, Miss Coutts apparently made another attempt to achieve a rapprochement between the Dickenses, but he replied that

in the last two years, I have been stabbed to death too often and too deep, not to have a settled knowledge of the wounded place.

It is simply impossible that such a thing can be. That figure is out of my life for evermore (except to darken it), and my desire is *never* to see it again.

Miss Coutts continued to show a keen interest in Charley, her informal godson, making gifts of three and five thousand pounds to him in his mid-twenties, and when another son, Walter, died in India on New Year's Eve 1863, she tried again to bring about reconciliation between the grieving parents, but Dickens was adamant. On 12 February 1864, he wrote to her:

I cannot tell you, my Dearest Friend – and I know I need not, with what feelings I received your affectionate letter this morning, or how dearly I prize it ... Do not think me unimpressed by certain words in your letter concerning forgiveness and tenderness when I say that I do not claim to have anything to forgive – that, if I had, I hope and believe I would forgive freely – but a page in my life that once had writing on it, has become absolutely blank, and ... it is not in my power to pretend that it has a solitary word on it'.

After that, Miss Coutts appears to have made no more attempts at reconciliation.

And what became of Urania Cottage? The publicity surrounding his marriage break-up – much of it of Dickens's own making – and the attendant scurrilous rumours made it impossible for him to continue with the project. He would not have wanted to embarrass Miss Coutts by a close association with him under such circumstances, and he nominated Henry Wills to succeed him as secretary. Wills was Dicken's deputy at *All the Year Round*, the journal he founded in 1859 after breaking with the publishers of *Household Words*, and had already been helping with this and other of Dickens's charitable activities. Other supporters of Urania Cottage continued to help, but without Dickens the heart had gone out of the project and the refuge closed in 1862, when the last women had been placed.

Had it been a success? Certainly, it was not all plain sailing. Girls will be girls. Isabella Gordon was dismissed for 'disturbing the general peace' with false and malicious complaints. Hannah Myers's 'malignity against the matrons was very intense and passionate'. Harriet Morson did a bunk through the fence, Mary Ann Shadwell through a pantry window. Julia Morley was suspected of some 'communication' with a local brickmaker, and 'all brickmakers are supposed to be prowling vagabonds'. Anna Maria Sesina, 'the perfect and most deceitful little minx', had to be expelled because 'she would have corrupted a nunnery in a fortnight'. Jemma Hiscock forced open the door to the beer cellar 'and drank until she was drunk, when she used the most horrible language and made a very repulsive exhibition of herself'. Isabella Garden was expelled with half a crown for a night's lodging 'and it was quite impossible to say what she might or might not do'.

Nevertheless, the first three emigrant girls left Gravesend in January 1849 bound for Australia on the sailing ship *Calcutta*, and by the time Urania Cottage closed its doors in 1862, an estimated one hundred fallen and destitute young women had passed through its doors.[29]

CHAPTER 5

Actress

It was Angela Burdett-Coutts who unwittingly triggered Dickens's first meeting with young actress Ellen Ternan in the summer of 1857.

Miss Coutts was a great patron of the arts and benefactress to actors. She owed her own vast wealth to the generosity of her stepmother, a former actress. But she was never quite comfortable with Dickens's taking part in theatrical performances: partly, because it tired him; partly, because she thought it a touch unseemly. So when the prospect arose of a public performance of a play that he and his family had previously put on in private, or at least semi-private, Miss Coutts advised that Katey, Mamey and Georgy be spared public exposure, and that their parts be given to professional actresses. One of those actresses would be young Ellen Ternan, less than half Dickens's age. Making her acquaintance would change his life forever.

The melodrama was *The Frozen Deep*, written by Wilkie Collins in close collaboration with Dickens, and the friends took the two male leads.

The plot took its inspiration from the real-life drama of Sir John Franklin who, after his recall as Lieutenant-Governor of Van Diemen's Land (Tasmania) in 1843, resumed his earlier career as an Arctic explorer. In 1845, he embarked on what would be his final voyage, in search of the North West Passage, the fabled waterway believed to connect the North Atlantic and Pacific Oceans, providing a navigable – and commercially profitable – channel that would accelerate the trade route from West to East. Franklin's expedition failed in circumstances that were never quite clear (rumours of cannibalism still persisted at the time the play was written). Some forty expeditions were sent out in search of him, and much valuable information on the region was obtained as a result. Dickens was fascinated by the Franklin story, which had inspired several other works. The central theme of *The Frozen Deep* was of a noble Arctic explorer, Richard Wardour (Dickens) heroically sacrificing his life to save that of his rival in love, Frank Aldersley (Collins) so that Aldersley could marry the girl of his dreams.

The play was first performed in January for invited guests in the little theatre at Tavistock House, with Katey taking the female lead and Mamey, Georgy and other family members playing smaller parts. Also in the cast was Wilkie Collins's younger brother Charles (future husband of Katey), while the artist Augustus Egg (who later proposed marriage to Georgy) played the part of the ship's cook. Dickens was manager and producer as well as the hero of the piece.

The Frozen Deep was so enthusiastically received by family and friends that a decision was made to revive it that summer and to stage a few performances at the Royal Gallery of Illustration, an intimate 500–seat performance venue in London's Regent Street. The play was a great success, delighting, among others, Queen Victoria, Prince Leopold of the Belgians and Prince Fredrick of Prussia. As a result, Dickens was invited to take the play to the Free Trade Hall in Manchester in August 1857.

Nelly Ternan

Dickens's friend, the playwright Douglas Jerrold, had recently died, leaving a widow and daughter. The Manchester shows provided the opportunity to raise funds for the benefit of Jerrold's family, as well as giving Dickens a creative challenge at a time when he was in dire need of a distraction from growing discontent at home.

The question was: who was to play the female parts? Miss Coutts had advised Dickens against using his female relatives and, in any case, their untrained voices were unlikely to be strong enough to project to the back of an auditorium the size of the Free Trade Hall.

So, in early August 1857, Dickens found himself travelling north to Manchester to audition a trio of professional actresses recommended to him by another friend, the playwright Alfred Wigan. The candidates were Frances Ternan, a respected actress from an established acting family, and the younger two of her three daughters: Maria, aged twenty, and Ellen (Nelly), aged eighteen. The eldest daughter Frances (Fanny) was already in work that summer.

Mrs Ternan had been a widow for many years. Her late husband, Thomas was an Irish-born actor and theatre manager with pretensions to gentility but only a mediocre talent. He had never been as successful as his wife, on whom fell most of the burden of earning a living for the family. She was therefore better prepared to cope than most when, in 1846, Thomas died in Bethnal Green Asylum of syphilis, or 'general paralysis of the insane' as it was called at the time.

Mrs Ternan first appeared on stage as a babe in arms with her mother and had been in steady, if unspectacular, work since her formal debut as an adult actress in 1815. But in the summer of 1857, there was little cause for optimism in the Ternan ménage: she, Maria and Nelly were all 'resting' and Fanny was engaged for a short run only. At fifty-five, Mrs Ternan must have wondered how much longer she could command leading roles and none of her girls showed much promise. The only date in the acting diary was an engagement in Doncaster in September. The chance of working with a celebrity such as Dickens must, therefore, have seemed an extremely attractive proposition.

The audition went well. Dickens took to the Ternan women and a contract was agreed: in *The Frozen Deep*, Mrs Ternan would play the old nurse, and Nelly and Maria the parts originally played by Katey and Georgy respectively. Maria and Nelly were also retained to perform in the farce *Uncle John* by John Buckstone, which was to round off the evenings at the Free Trade Hall. Nelly, who had already appeared earlier in the year in the Buckstone burlesque *Atalanta*, was to take the part previously played by Katey. *Uncle John* tells the tale of an old man infatuated by his young ward. Dickens had originally played the old man and Katey the ward, intending to hand his part over to a friend for the Manchester performances. He met Nelly and he changed his mind. And so it began.

Dickens supervised the rehearsals for *The Frozen Deep* in his usual clear, indefatigable and relentlessly methodical manner. When the acting party set off for Manchester on 20 August, they were quietly confident of success.

Manchester was the place to be that summer. Cottonopolis was heaving with visitors to the Art Treasures Exhibition. The show ran for six months, attracted 1.3 million visitors, displayed 16,000 works of art, including 1,100 Old Masters. It remains the biggest art event ever held in Britain, attracting royalty, politicians and celebrities from throughout Europe, as well as bringing high culture to the masses. The week that Dickens attended the show at the end of July, other visitors included novelist Elizabeth Gaskell, who complained that her summer was ruined by the sheer number of acquaintances who came to stay in order to visit the exhibition. It may well have been the draw of the exhibition that persuaded Dickens that Manchester would be an ideal venue for the play.[1]

The Manchester benefit performances of *The Frozen Deep* were both a popular and a critical success, and the play was held over for a third night to meet demand. By the end of the long weekend, Dickens had established that the Ternans would be appearing on stage in Doncaster in a few weeks' time.

Back at Gad's Hill, Dickens was agitated and unable to settle, unnerved by his discovery of Nelly Ternan.

Dickens was forty-five years old to Nelly's eighteen. He was a self-made man, the greatest novelist of his age, a tireless journalist, social reformer, commentator, editor, theatrical patron, doer of good works, apparent pillar of society and father of nine. Middle-aged he might be, but he was still upright, stylish, flamboyant even – in dress and manner – with his eccentric coiffure and exotic waistcoats. He was impetuous and interested in everybody and everything. He was often charming and equally often moody and irritable, particularly when he was writing.

Nelly was a shapely, blonde, blue-eyed slip of a girl, pretty and spirited, but with no great acting talent. Fatherless and penniless, she was poor but she was honest. Above all, she was young. And Dickens had a dread of growing old. In Nelly, he saw the perfect opportunity to keep himself connected to youth, to reinvent himself on a new stage.

In his agitation, Dickens persuaded his friend Wilkie Collins to accompany him on a trip. 'I want to escape from myself,' he explained, 'my blankness is inconceivable – indescribable – my misery, amazing.'

Ostensibly the trip was to be a simple walking tour through Cumberland and Yorkshire. In reality, it was a way of staying away from home and it had but one destination: mid-September in Doncaster, where the Ternans would next appear on stage.

Dickens fictionalized the trip as *The Lazy Tour of Two Idle Apprentices*. The travelogue includes tales told by fellow-travellers whom the apprentices meet on their journey. One is a grim gothic yarn in which an older man extorts a young woman's fortune (having been spurned by her mother, who married his rival) and then effectively bullies her to death by sheer willpower – by simply willing her repeatedly, to her face, to die.

About this time Dickens confided in Forster that it was increasingly clear that he and Catherine, his wife of over twenty years, were not, after all, made for each other, and that 'what is now befalling, I have seen steadily coming'. Dickens should have had everything he wanted in life, but the feeling that haunted him all his life – that something was missing – remained as strong as ever.

What Mrs Ternan and her daughters thought when Dickens and Collins fetched up in Doncaster is not recorded, but they must have wondered at the happy coincidence that brought a distinguished acquaintance such as Dickens to an undistinguished venue such as Doncaster just when Nelly and Maria were performing in undistinguished dramas.

If Dickens was going to indulge in a serious romantic liaison – and although his reunion with the former Maria Beadnell proved a disaster, it had nevertheless rekindled tender memories of early passion – it was unsurprising that he fell in love with an actress.

Dickens had loved acting all his life, from his childhood days at Chatham when his father would lift him and Fanny onto a table at the Mitre Inn to perform their party pieces. His early enthusiasm was reinforced by theatre visits with his father or his cousin, James Lamert. He staged sketches at his school, Wellington House, and produced private theatricals at his parents' home.

As a young man, he had ambitions to become a professional actor before journalism took over his life. His first play, *Is She His Wife?*, was produced at St James's Theatre in 1837, when he was just twenty-five years old. He regularly performed in, produced and directed amateur theatricals in London and the provinces. In 1851, he organized amateur performances at Rockingham Castle, the home of his friends Lavinia and Richard Watson. The same year he directed and acted in Edward Bulwer-Lytton's play *Not So Bad as We Seem* at Devonshire House in aid of the Guild of Literature and Art, which he and Bulwer-Lytton had recently founded for the benefit of authors and artists; and he went on a northern tour with the play in 1852, by which time the family were living at Tavistock House, where the schoolroom was converted into a private theatre. Then there were the public readings, which began tentatively with *A Christmas Carol* in Birmingham in late December 1853. The readings programme began in earnest in April 1858, just as his relationship with Nelly was being established.

Meeting Nelly Ternan provided the perfect opportunity for Dickens to create a role he had longed to inhabit since the death of his sister-in-law Mary. He now had the chance to become the protector and lover – platonic or otherwise – of an innocent young girl, and the sponsor of her widowed mother and fatherless sisters. 'I wish I had been born in the days of ogres and dragon-guarded castles,' he wrote to Lavinia Watson in December 1857, by which time the marital separation process had begun its messy course.

I wish an ogre with seven heads ... had taken the princess whom I adore – you have no idea how intensely I love her! – to his stronghold on the top of a high series of mountains, and there tied her up by the hair. Nothing would suit me half so well this day, as climbing after her, sword in hand, and either winning her or being killed.

He wrote in similar vein to Lady Duff Gordon four weeks later.

One of the most restless of men at all times, I am at such a crisis worse than ever. Nothing would satisfy at this present writing, but the having to go up a tremendous mountain, magic spell in one hand and sword in the other, to find the girl of my heart (whom I never did find), surrounded by fifty dragons – kill them all, and bear her off, triumphant. I might finish the story in the usual way, by settling down and living happy ever afterwards – perhaps; I am not sure even of that.

How long it took Dickens to win over his 'princess' (and her mother) is uncertain, but in 1859, having dispatched Mrs Ternan and Fanny to Italy at his own expense to further Fanny's singing career, he bought the lease on Houghton House at Ampthill Place in London, where he installed Maria and Nelly. Initially, the lease was held in the names of Nelly's sisters, but it was transferred to Nelly when she came of age the following year. It was the consolidation of a relationship that endured thirteen years until Dickens's death and remained throughout shrouded in secrecy, subterfuge and cover-up.

When Dickens took up with Nelly Ternan, he took on the whole Ternan family, presumably out of a combination of guilt, generosity and enlightened self-interest. There is no better place to hide a mistress than in the bosom of her own family, with mother and sisters acting as chaperones when propriety required it, but fading discreetly into the background when expediency required it more.

What did Mrs Ternan think about the arrangement? The indications are that she was a respectable woman who brought up her daughters to be likewise; but widowed as she was at an early age by the death of a husband who died of syphilis, and struggling to keep her daughters, she may have wondered whether respectability was worth it. The prospect of material security for all her girls – and that prospect would be fully realized in different ways, thanks to the Dickens connection – must have seemed an attractive proposition, particularly if the appearance of respectability could be maintained and reputations compromised as little as possible. And Dickens was as keen about this as anyone.

Precisely what happened to Nelly for the next few years is unclear. Dickens burned his private papers in 1860, and again in 1869; his diaries he destroyed on an annual basis.[2] However, Nelly's leading biographer, in an extensive forensic analysis of the available evidence, suggests the following as the most likely narrative:

That Nelly became pregnant by Dickens and that, to minimize the possibility of scandal, he moved her to France, probably somewhere in the Paris area; that she had her baby there, with her mother in attendance, some time in 1862; that the baby died, probably during the summer of 1863; and that she then stayed on in France, or spent most of her time abroad until June 1865.[3]

Dickens had always loved visiting France, where his work enjoyed great success, but the pattern of his visits changed dramatically in the summer of 1862, when there was a veritable flurry of cross-Channel trips – eight round trips in all – before he settled in Paris for a protracted period. One reason he gave was his anxiety over Georgy's apparent ill-health. She was suffering a 'sudden decline of the health and spirit' and 'labouring under degeneration of the heart', he wrote to the actor Daniel Macready, and Paris would provide a couple of months of complete change. There has been a suggestion that Georgy's illness was psychosomatic as a result of being upstaged by Nelly; certainly, she made a complete recovery.

Moreover, Dickens knew in advance when his French sojourn would be over: not until the middle of February, he told his sister Letitia. To Wilkie Collins he wrote: 'Who knows but that towards the end of February, I might be open to any foreign proposal whatsoever. Distance no object; climate of no importance.' The end of an illness can hardly be predicted with such accuracy, but the outcome of pregnancy can.

It also remains a fact that Dickens's daughter Katey confided to her biographer that he and Nelly had a child – a son – who died in infancy, a fact confirmed later by her brother Harry. What possible reason might his children have had to lie?

Nelly and her mother, with Dickens in attendance, returned to England from France on the afternoon of 9 June 1865. They travelled up to London through Kent on the tidal express train from Folkestone, so called because its schedule depended on tide times in the Channel and therefore varied slightly from day to day. On the line was a gang of workmen hurrying to replace plates on the track before the train passed over the bridge on the river Beult, near Staplehurst. The foreman thought it was Saturday. In fact it was Friday. As a result, the train arrived before he was expecting it, while the plates were still loose.

At 3 p.m., the tidal express left the rails at the bridge, broke in two, and eight first-class carriages plunged from the bridge into the river below, where they remained on their side, twisted and flattened. The carriage in which Dickens and the Ternans were travelling hung suspended in the air over the side of the bridge. Dickens was unhurt, but ten passengers were killed and fourteen seriously injured. Among them was Nelly, who is believed to have suffered a broken arm, but who was quickly whisked away from the scene with her mother, to save Dickens further embarrassment.

Once they were safely dispatched, Dickens began to help the injured. Armed with a bottle of brandy and a hat full of drinking water, he moved among the injured and the dying for several hours before a trained medical team arrived at the scene of the accident on special trains. He wrote to his friend, Miss Coutts:

I worked hard afterwards among the dead and the dying and it is that shock – not the shock of the stumbling carriage, which was nothing – that I feel a little. I could not have imagined so appalling a scene.

Three days later, Dickens had composed himself sufficiently to address the Head Station Master at Charing Cross on the relatively prosaic subject of some jewellery (presumably gifts from him) that Nelly had lost in the crash. He wrote:

A lady who was in the carriage with me in the terrible accident on Friday lost, in the struggle of being got out of the carriage, a gold watch-chain with a smaller gold watch-chain attached, a bundle of charms, a gold watch-key and a gold seal engraved 'Ellen'.

I promised the lady to make her loss known at headquarters, in case these trinkets should be found.[4]

From the period immediately after the crash, some three dozen or so letters survive in which Dickens described, in

greater or lesser detail, the events of the afternoon of the crash.
All of them stress his involvement in the rescue work, increasingly so as time goes by. The longest is to his old friend Thomas
Mitton, which includes an account that acknowledges, without
admitting their identities, the presence in the carriage with
him of Nelly and her mother. By now, Dickens had refined
the account into the perfect dramatic narrative, complete with
dialogue, and with himself in the role of hero of the hour.

I am a little shaken, not by the beating and dragging of the carriage in
which I was, but by the hard work afterwards in getting out the dying
and the dead, which was most horrible.

I was in the only carriage that did not go over into the stream. It
was caught upon the turn by some of the ruin of the bridge, and hung
suspended and balanced in an apparently impossible manner. Two
ladies were my fellow passengers; an old one, and a young one. This is
exactly what passed: you may judge from it the precise length of the
suspense. Suddenly we were off the rail and beating the ground as the
car of a half-emptied balloon might. The old lady cried out 'My God'
and the young one screamed. I caught hold of them both (the old lady
sat opposite, and the young one on my left), and said: 'We can't help
ourselves, but we can be quiet and composed. Pray don't cry out.'

The old lady immediately answered: 'Thank you. Rely upon me.
Upon my soul, I will be quiet.' The young lady said in a frantic way, 'Let
us join hands and die friends.' We were then all tilted down together in
a corner of the carriage, and stopped, I said to them thereupon: 'You
may be sure nothing worse can happen. Our danger must be over. Will
you remain here without stirring, while I get out of the window.' They
both answered quite collectedly: yes, and I got out without the least
notion what had happened.

Fortunately, I got out with great caution and stood upon the step.
Looking down, I saw the bridge gone and nothing below me but the
line of rail. Some people in the two other compartments were madly
trying to plunge out at the window, and had no idea that there was
an open swampy field 15 feet below them and nothing else! The two
guards (one with his face cut) were running up and down on the

down side of the bridge (which was not torn up) quite wildly. I called out to them: 'Look at me. Do stop an instant and look at me, and tell me whether you don't know me.' One of them answered: 'We know you very well, Mr Dickens'. 'Then,' I said, 'my good fellow for God's sake give me your key, and send one of those labourers here, and I'll empty this carriage.' We did it quite safely, by means of a plank or two, and when it was done I saw all the rest of the train except the two baggage cars down in the stream. I got into the carriage again for my brandy flask, took off my travelling hat for a basin, climbed down the brickwork and filled my hat with water. I came upon a staggering man covered with blood (I think he must have been flung clean out of his carriage) with such a frightful cut across the skull that I couldn't bear to look at him. I poured some water over his face, and gave him some to drink, and gave him some brandy, and laid him down on the grass, and he said: 'I am gone' and died afterwards. Then I stumbled over a lady lying on her back against a little pollard tree, with the blood streaming over her face (which was lead colour) in a number of distinct little streams from the head. I asked if she could swallow a little brandy, and she just nodded, and I gave her some and left her for somebody else. The next time I passed her, she was dead. Then a man examined at the inquest yesterday (who evidently had not the least remembrance of what really passed) came running up to me and implored me to help him find his wife, who was afterwards found dead. No imagination can conceive the ruin of the carriages, or the extraordinary weights under which the people were lying, or the complications into which they were twisted up among iron and wood, and mud and water.

I don't want to be examined at the inquest, and I don't want to write about it. It could do no good either way. And I could only seem to speak about myself. Which, of course I would rather not do. I am keeping very quiet here. I have a – I don't know what to call it – constitutional (I suppose) presence of mind, and was not in the least fluttered at the time. I instantly remembered that I had [a] manuscript with me, and clambered back into the carriage for it. But in writing these scanty words of recollection I feel the shake and am obliged to stop.[5]

Back in London, Dickens was concerned that Nelly

– henceforth known as 'the patient' – should be cosseted. He instructed his man Thompson to take to her all sorts of food delicacies: 'a little basket of fresh fruit, a jar of clotted cream … and a chicken, a pair of pigeons or some nice little bird.' Also on Wednesday and Friday mornings, he should take to her some things of the same sort, 'making a little variety each day.'

In 1866, the year after Nelly returned to England, her sister Fanny married the newly widowed Thomas Trollope, brother of the more famous Anthony. Fanny, who had gone to Italy some years previously, at Dickens's expense, to take singing lessons, had given up her full-time commitment to opera in order to teach Italian and music, and had been invited to Trollope's home in Florence to act as governess to his thirteen-year-old daughter. Within months, Tom and Fanny were engaged to be married. The age difference between them was comparable to that between Nelly and Dickens: she was thirty-one and he was fifty-six. Nevertheless, it seems to have been a happy arrangement and Fanny settled comfortably into life at the Trollope villa in Florence.

Three years earlier, her sister Maria had wed a solid young man from a respectable Oxford brewing family. Her marriage was less successful but she found her consolation in foreign travel, particularly after Fanny was installed in Florence. While Maria worked to establish herself as an artist and journalist, Fanny continued to pursue her literary career, with the serialization of her first novel appearing in Dickens's magazine, *All the Year Round.*

The openings and contacts that Dickens's patronage brought Fanny and Maria enabled them to put behind them the persona of actress – at which neither of them had particularly excelled, despite Dickens's best efforts to promote them – and to glide into more refined literary and artistic circles than they might have expected, given their provenance. To some extent, there came a point at which Nelly, the initiator of all this largesse, was overtaken by the good fortune of her sisters. They had husbands, respectable positions in society, and careers as well. Nelly had Dickens and no prospect of anything more while Catherine Dickens lived.[6] While her sisters led real and interesting lives, Nelly waited for Dickens to visit.

Did Dickens and Nelly make each other happy? The answer is: probably not as much as they might have hoped. Nelly lived in a gilded cage, while Dickens exchanged a wife who did not share his life – for whatever reasons – for a mistress who could not share it, if appearances of respectability were to be maintained. It can surely be no coincidence that, in the novels written after Dickens met Nelly Ternan, a new type of heroine emerged. The long-suffering ones are still there, but they are joined by the likes of feisty little Lucie Manette (*A Tale of Two Cities*), wilful Bella Wilfer (*Our Mutual Friend*) and, above all, the enchanting but cold-hearted Estella Magwitch (*Great Expectations*).

In the early part of 1867, Dickens and Nelly were making plans to move her from a cottage in Slough to a villa in the then semi-rural suburb of Peckham in south London. The reason that a larger house was needed may have been because Nelly was again pregnant. The hint comes in two brief entries in Dickens's one surviving diary. On 13 April, he entered the word 'Arrival' and on 20 April, he entered the word 'Loss'. That there was a second child that died seems a feasible interpretation. As Tomalin points out:

Purely on the basis of probability, as association of 13 years between a man who had fathered children regularly on his wife over a period of

16 years and a healthy young woman who had no difficulty conceiving children later might be expected to produce children.[7]

The reading tour of the USA between November 1867 and April 1868 was Dickens's first trip to that country since his four-month visit in 1842. Initially, he hoped to get Nelly to join him. To this end, he left his deputy, Harry Wills with instructions to this effect, dependent on a coded message that Dickens would send to Wills on his arrival. In the event, he decided that it could not be; instead, Nelly and her mother were encouraged to go to Florence to stay with Fanny, until he returned to England.

The American trip proved a great success. This was just as well, since Dickens needed the money. By this time he had multiple households to maintain: Nelly's, his own at Gad's Hill and his wife Catherine's at Gloucester Crescent. Among other family commitments, he had taken on financial responsibility for the widow and children of his brother Alfred, and for the abandoned wife and children of his brother Augustus, who ran off to the States and started another family there. Meanwhile Anna, the wife of his brother Frederick, was taking advantage of the new 1857 Divorce Act to part company with her husband.

So it was fortunate that Dickens made a profit of £19,000 for his seventy-six readings in the States, which were attended by over 100,000 people. However, it was a punishing schedule for a man in his mid-fifties, and he was forced through ill-health and exhaustion to curtail many of the social events planned for him. Some said the US trip nearly killed him.

Financial considerations apart, one consolation of the American trip was that he was able to renew his friendship with Annie Fields and her husband James, Dickens's Boston publisher, whom he had first met during their European trip of

1859–60, an experience they would repeat a decade later. Annie Fields was devoted to Dickens, whom she called The Great Enchanter; he, in turn, confided to her some of the problems of his emotional life, and his friendship with Nelly. She sensed an underlying feeling of 'gloom' in Dickens, a great sorrow lurking just beneath his jolly exterior. 'It is wonderful the fun and flow of spirits C.D. has,' she wrote in her diary, 'for he is a sad man.'[8]

Not all Mrs Fields' literati friends share her enthusiasm for Dickens. While acknowledging the man's 'restlessness, his terrible sadness', Henry Longfellow complained that 'Dickens saved himself for his books; there was nothing to be learned in private'. Ralph Waldo Emerson told her:

I am afraid he has too much talent for his genius; it is a fearful locomotive to which he is bound and can never be free from it or set it rest. You see him quite wrong, evidently, and would persuade me that he is a genial creature, full of sweetness and amenities, and superior to his talents, but I fear he is harnessed to them. He is too consummate an artist to have a thread of nature left. He daunts me! I have not the key.[9]

When Dickens set off back to England, Mrs Fields was bereft. 'I feel somehow like one of his daughters,' she wrote in her diary, 'as if I could not take too great care of him.'

Dickens had already conducted reading tours in England before he left for the States; and, undeterred by indifferent health, he was back on the UK reading circuit by October 1868, but this time it was clearly billed as his farewell tour. In January 1869, he added to his programme the famous scene from *Oliver Twist* in which Bill Sikes brutally beats Nancy to death, a murder that Dickens acted out with such intensity as to leave his audiences utterly transfixed, and his friends seriously worried. They were right to be worried for, fifteen weeks into the tour, it had to be abandoned because Dickens became seriously ill.

By early 1870, Dickens was beginning to feel old. 'At times there was a weariness about him,' Katey wrote. Despite the way he felt, 'he kept up with his spirits and went on with his work,'[10] for as he once said to Forster, in the dark time before his separation from Catherine: 'It is much better to go on and fret, than to stop and fret.'

On Friday 2 June, he returned from his London office to Gad's Hill, where he was joined on Sunday by Katey, who came to talk to her father about going on the stage to earn some extra money. She had already been offered work by an impresario who had seen her in *The Frozen Deep* all those years ago. 'We will talk about it when the others have gone to bed,' he told her.

'I shall never forget that talk,' Katey told her biographer. 'With great earnestness my father dissuaded me from going on the stage. "You are pretty and no doubt would do well, but you are too sensitive a nature to bear the brunt of much you would encounter. Although there are nice people on the stage, there are some who would make your hair stand on end. You are clever enough to do something else." He finally dismissed the subject by saying, "I will make it up to you".'

He went on to speak of other subjects – with regret. He wished, he said, that he had been 'a better father – a better man'. He talked and talked, *how* he talked, until three o'clock in the morning, when we parted for bed. I know things about my father's character that no-one else ever knew; he was not a good man, but he was not a fast man, but he was wonderful! He fell in love with this girl, I did not blame *her* – it is never one person's fault.[11]

The following morning, when Katey went to say goodbye to her father, he was particularly affectionate. As she left, something called her back, and she returned to embrace him once again. It was the last time she would see him conscious.

Dickens with his daughters, Mamey and Katey

For the next couple of days he seemed in good spirits, eager to finish the next episode of his latest novel, *The Mystery of Edwin Drood*. But, one evening at dinner, Georgy

perceived a marked change in the colour and expression of his face. When she asked him if he was feeling ill, he replied: 'Yes very ill – for the last hour.' He declined her suggestion that a doctor be sent for. As time passed, it became obvious that a fit was coming on … when his sister-in-law … entreated him to let her assist him to his room that he might lie down. 'Yes – on the ground,' he instantly replied. Struggling from … the chair to his feet, he took her arm. From which he slipped to the carpet, where he lay unconscious. The servants lifted him on to a sofa brought from the drawing-room, wrapped a rug around him and gently placed pillows beneath his head.[12]

A local doctor was sent for, and Katey and Mamey were recalled to Gad's Hill.

Directly we entered the house I could hear my father's deep breathing. All through the night we watched, taking it in turns to place hot bricks at his feet, which were so cold. But he did not stir.[13]

Dickens's eldest son Charley arrived the next morning with a second doctor, but their joint opinion was that Dickens was beyond all human help. Just before six o'clock, his breathing became less, 'a tear rose to his right eye and trickled down his cheek'. And with that, Charles Dickens was gone. He was just fifty-eight years old. Katey went up to London to break the news to her mother. In the afternoon, Nelly Ternan arrived. In the evening, Katey's friend, the artist John Millais, arrived to sketch Dickens's likeness.

Dickens told Forster he always hoped to die 'in harness'. That, at least, was granted him. Katey said no one would have wished him back, 'as he would not have desired to live and grow old; he had a certain distaste (reminiscent of his mother) to be regarded as growing old.'[14] That, at least, was spared him. Annie Fields wrote: 'I thank God afresh that he is no longer in a world which held so much pain for him.'

Many years before, Dickens expressed a wish to be buried next to his beloved sister-in-law Mary. In 1837, he had purchased a plot at the new Kensal Green cemetery, where she was interred, but in the event her brother was buried next to her. To Forster, he then expressed a preference for some modest resting-place 'in the small graveyard under Rochester Castle wall', background to the happy days of his childhood, or perhaps 'in the little churches of Cobham or Shorne'.[15]

Dickens had a horror of false sentimentality in death. In response to an invitation from his sister Letitia to attend the funeral of her husband Henry's cousin – their adopted son – he had written a letter full of love, condolence, sympathy and compassion, but added:

I have the greatest objection to attend a funeral in which my affections are not strongly and immediately concerned. I have no notion of a funeral as a matter of form or ceremony. And just as I should expressly prohibit the summoning to my own burial, of anyone who was not very near or dear to me, so I revolt from myself appearing at that solemn rite, unless the deceased were very near or dear to me. I cannot endure being dressed up by an undertaker as part of his trade-show. I was not in this poor good fellow's house in his lifetime, and I feel I have no business there when he lies dead in it. My mind is penetrated with sympathy and compassion for the young widow, but that feeling is a real thing, and my attendance as a mourner would not be – to myself. I know full well that you cannot delegate to me your memories of and associations with the deceased: and the more true and tender they are, the more invincible is my objection to become a form in the midst of the most awful realities.

Dickens was quite clear about what sort of funeral he did *not* want for himself.[16] In his handwritten will, dated 12 May 1869, just over a year before he died, he wrote:

I emphatically direct that I be buried in an inexpensive, unostentatious, and strictly private manner; that no public announcement be made of the time or place of my burial; that at the utmost not more than three plain mourning coaches be employed; and that those who attend my funeral wear no scarf, cloak, black bow, long hat-band, or other such revolting absurdity. I direct that my name be inscribed in plain English letters on my tomb, without the addition of 'Mr' or 'Esquire'. I conjure my friends on no account to make me the subject of any monument, memorial or testimony whatever. I rest my claims to the remembrance of my country upon my published works, and to the remembrances of my friends upon their remembrance of me.[17]

His public thought otherwise, however, and a compromise was reached between Westminster Abbey and the executors of Dickens's will, Georgy Hogarth and John Forster. As *The Times* newspaper reported:

It was found, on opening Mr. Dickens's will that, although his instructions were explicit in forbidding all pomp and show … he had named no place of burial; and therefore his executors felt that it was open to them to concur with the national wish, if they could only insure secrecy as to place and time.[18]

'The wish of the people has prevailed,' the newspaper reported the day after the funeral, 'and Charles Dickens rests in the Abbey Church of St. Peter at Westminster.'

Our readers will learn with surprise and satisfaction that the funeral of the great novelist was celebrated at an early hour yesterday morning in Poets' Corner, with as much privacy as could have been secured for it in any little village church in Kent, or even in Wales or Cornwall. A grave had been dug during the night, and we believe that we are right in asserting that, besides the Dean and Canons, hardly a member of the Cathedral body on Monday evening was aware of the intended arrangement. It appears that some days ago the Dean sent a communication to the family of Mr Dickens to the effect that, if it was desired by themselves or by the public that he should be buried in the Abbey, he would do all in his power to facilitate the arrangements.

And so it happened. At an early hour on the day of the funeral, 'almost before anyone was stirring', the coffin left Gad's Hill Place for a local station, from where it was forwarded to London's Charing Cross station on a special train, arriving at nine o'clock.

In a few minutes more the hearse, which was plainness itself, was on its way down Whitehall to the Abbey, followed by the mourning coaches, as we believe that not a single person of the many scores who must have met the gloomy cavalcade as it slowly paced along was aware that the hearse was conveying to its last resting-place all that was mortal of Charles Dickens.

Shortly before half-past nine, the cortege entered Dean's Yard and the plain oak coffin was carried through the cloisters to the door of the nave, where it was met by the Dean. There was no choir, no hymns, no psalms; only the organ playing at intervals. It was a simple funeral. When it was over, the Clerk of Works cast earth into the grave, 'the mourners, 14 in number ... gathered round the grave to take a last look at the coffin which held the great novelist's remains'. They placed wreaths of *immortelles* and other flowers on the coffin lid, and, with that, the service was at an end. Honour was satisfied on both sides: the funeral was private but, afterwards, the grave was left open for visitors during the day; and the following Sunday, the Dean preached a funeral sermon on Dickens's career and character for all who cared to attend. At one o'clock the bell of Rochester Cathedral was tolled to mark Dickens's passing.

No journalist from *The Times* was, in fact, at the burial service at Westminster Abbey. The newspaper's report was written by its leader writer, William Stebbing, from notes begun by Forster and completed – when Forster, already in poor health, became apparently too upset and overwhelmed to continue – by Wilkie Collins. The report mentioned fourteen mourners present. It also listed those in the three mourning coaches as follows. In the first coach were four of Dickens's children: Charley Dickens, Harry Dickens, Mamey Dickens and Katey Collins. In the second coach were his sister-in-law Georgy Hogarth, his sister Letitia Austin, Charley's wife Bessie Dickens and John Forster. In the third coach were his doctor Frank Beard, Katey's husband Charles Collins and his brother Wilkie Collins, Dickens's nephew Edmund Dickens, and his solicitor, Frederic Ouvry.

That makes thirteen mourners, one less than in *The Times* report. One can only assume that the fourteenth mystery mourner was Nelly Ternan, and that one of the reasons that Dickens wanted a quiet, private funeral was to make sure that she would be able to attend.[19]

For several days after Dickens's burial, the public came in their thousands to pay their last respects.

Then there was the will. One of the most striking elements of Dickens's last will and testament is that the first named beneficiary is Nelly Ternan and the last his wife Catherine.

Nelly was left a thousand pounds, although it is likely that ample provision had been made for her discreetly during Dickens's lifetime.[20] In the will, Dickens gave her address, disingenuously, as 'late of Houghton Place, Ampthill Square', the house he had acquired for her in 1859. Catherine was to receive the interest on eight thousand pounds, to be invested for her by her sons. He could not resist adding, quite gratuitously, that she had received from him during his life an annual income of six hundred pounds, 'while all the great charges of a numerous and expensive family have devolved entirely upon myself'.[21] Forster was left the manuscripts of all Dickens's published works; and Georgy received eight thousand pounds plus personal items and all Dickens's private papers, together with 'my grateful blessing as the best and truest friend man ever had'.[22]

Individual small bequests were made to servants and appropriate provisions were made for other children. Mamey received one thousand pounds plus an annual allowance of three hundred pounds while she remained unmarried; and in a late codicil to the will added just a week before his father's death, Charley inherited Dickens's interest in the weekly journal *All the Year Round*, as well as his collection of books, engravings and prints.

Georgy Hogarth and John Forster were appointed 'guardians of the persons of my children during their respective minorities', a duty that they executed admirably. 'And lastly,' Dickens wrote, in a final snub to his wife,

I solemnly enjoin my dear children always to remember how much they owe to the said Georgina Hogarth, and never be wanting in a grateful and affectionate attachment to her, for they know well that she has been, through all the stages of their growth and progress, their ever useful, self-denying friend.[23]

CHAPTER 6

Epilogue

Dying in 1863, Elizabeth Dickens predeceased her son by seven years. Like him, she was wilful and flamboyant almost to the end. When she finally slipped into senility, she was cared for, at Dickens's expense, by two young widows whose families also enjoyed Dickens's financial support. They were his sister Letitia Austin, whose architect husband Henry – once Dickens's rival for the affections of Maria Beadnell – died in 1861; and his sister-in-law Helen Dickens, whose husband Alfred, Dickens's most reliable and enterprising brother, died in 1860.

As for Maria Beadnell, her husband, Henry Winter was declared bankrupt in 1859. He took holy orders and was ordained as a vicar in Northumberland, where they lived until his death in 1871. Maria died in 1886 and was buried in the cemetery in Southsea.

Catherine Dickens survived her estranged husband by nine years. After their separation in 1858, she worked hard to keep up her social life. There were visits to the theatre, concerts, dinner parties and outings.[1] She was supported by many of Dickens's former friends, who were more inclined to take her part in the affair, including the Thackerays, the Lemons (Mark Lemon was the editor of *Punch* magazine), the Collinses, the Millais, and the Evanses, of Dickens's former publisher Bradbury and Evans, from whom he parted company when they declined to give space in *Punch* to his 'personal statement' on the marital separation.

In 1861, three years after the estrangement, Charley married the Evanses' daughter Bessie. Dickens refused to attend the wedding, denigrating the match as a big mistake. But Catherine quickly warmed to the young bride, whose eldest sister Margaret became one of her closest friends. She was delighted to become a grandmother; other friends invited her to become godmother to their child. She made a great effort to stay as close as possible to all her children; to those sons who emigrated, she wrote long and frequent letters for the rest of her life.

When Dickens died, Catherine was not invited to the very private funeral, at which Nelly Ternan may have been present. But she was gratified to receive a letter of condolence from Queen Victoria. After his death, she was able to re-establish herself as his widow, the materfamilias of the Dickens clan. When Charley bought his father's house at auction and Georgy and Mamey moved to a rented house near Hyde Park, Catherine was able to spend weeks at a time at Gad's Hill with her eldest son and his young family and to enjoy Christmases and other events in the bosom of the extended family from which Dickens, the 'father' of Christmas, had sought to exclude her.

Catherine died of cervical cancer in 1879. Towards the end, she was nursed by her daughter Katey, who endeavoured, with some success, to 'soften her remembrance' of Dickens. In retrospect, Katey felt regret that she had not taken her mother's part more forcefully during her lifetime.

One afternoon, when [Katey] was sitting by the bedside of her mother (who knew she was dying), she requested her to go to a drawer and bring a bundle of letters (there was also a locket containing a likeness of her husband and a lock of his hair) which her daughter placed upon the bed. Tenderly laying her hand upon the treasured missives, Mrs Dickens said with great earnestness: 'Give these to the British Museum – that the world may know that he loved me once'.[2]

Whether these letters did, in fact, prove Dickens's early devotion to his wife was the subject of some debate. When Katey first read them, she was herself unsure, suspecting they might suggest the opposite: that Dickens already found Catherine slightly tedious even before they married. She considered burning them but was dissuaded by George Bernard Shaw, who, not having read them, encouraged her to lodge them after all with the British Museum, where they would remain unpublished until after the death of the last surviving Dickens child, Henry, in 1933; they were then published in 1935 as *Mr & Mrs Charles Dickens: His Letters to Her*.

Katey also wrote a biography of her father, largely to exonerate her mother from the accusations made at the time of the separation, and also to assuage her guilt at having been neglectful of her mother for fear of angering her father; but she had second thoughts, and burnt it. However, she confided her memories to her friend and confidante, Gladys Storey, with instructions that they should be written up after her death. *Dickens and Daughter* was duly published in 1939. On reading it, Shaw wrote to Storey that he now realised that Dickens's letters to Catherine 'proved nothing at all … I was sorry I had not let her burn them. I should certainly have done so if I had read them.'[3]

When Storey's book came out, Dickensian loyalists suggested that Katey must have been senile to reveal details about her father that included anything negative, thus echoing the same charge of mental instability that Dickens had levelled against his wife in the 'violated' letter. Shaw took exception to this. Responding to a review of Storey's book in *The Times Literary Supplement* hinting at Katey's possible insanity, he rejected the idea outright, writing: 'The facts of the case are in bad taste. Facts often are. But either way, your reviewer will be glad to have them put right.'[4]

Katey, who had married Charles Collins in 1860, much to Dickens's dismay, was widowed in 1873. The following year she married fellow artist Charles (Carlo) Perugini and bore a son, who died in infancy. She was the only family member to divulge intimate information about Charles Dickens to a biographer. Ever her father's daughter, she remained impetuous and full of vigour until her death in 1929.

Georgy and Mamey continued to live together for a while. Neither married. Georgina, guardian of Dickens's public image until her death, helped Mamey 'edit' Dickens's letters for publication, a process which entailed suppressing anything which might reflect badly on the Inimitable one, thus producing a distorted, one-sided, excessively reverential account.

To Georgy's credit, she was assiduous in maintaining contacts between all the members of the Dickens family, particularly the younger generation, and she provided material support for his widowed and impoverished sister Letitia.

She also kept in touch with Maria Beadnell Winter and Nelly Ternan, although it has been suggested that, in the latter case, self-interest may have been a motive.

It can hardly have been an entirely straightforward relationship. It seems likely that Georgina was keeping something of a watchful eye on Nelly, hoping for a measure of control over any letters or revelations she might, at some point, be tempted to make.[5]

The same may have applied to her relationship with Maria Beadnell Winter. She successfully prevented Dickens's letters to Maria from being published in England (but not in America) until after her death. Georgy lived until 1917. Letitia died in 1893, Mamey and Maria in 1896.

Angela Burdett-Coutts, meanwhile, continued to devote her life and much of her fortune to good works, in recognition of which she was created a baroness in 1871. Little more than two years after the death in December 1878 of her former governess and 'poor darling' Harriet Brown, 'the companion and sunshine of my life for fifty-two years',[6] she married her American-born secretary, William Ashmead Bartlett (1851–1921), who would later become Conservative MP for Westminster. The bride was nearly sixty-seven years old, the groom less than half her age when they wed at Christchurch, Down Street, in February 1881, against the advice of many friends and to the dismay of Queen Victoria, who called it 'madness'.

She lived nearly another quarter of a century. The 'Queen of the Poor' died shortly before the end of 1906 and was buried in Westminster Abbey in early 1907. Her funeral was attended by the royal family, princes of the church and government leaders – but also by flower girls from Bermondsey and working men from Bethnal Green.[7]

Resourceful little Nelly Ternan, still just thirty-one years old when Dickens died in 1870, remained good friends with Georgina and Mamey, but otherwise reinvented herself completely. She took ten years off her age;[8] and, six years after Dickens's death, she married a young clergyman, George Wharton Robinson and became a pillar of polite society in Margate, a town on the Kent coast where her husband ran a boys' school and Nelly took to giving readings from Dickens.

They had two children: Geoffrey, born in 1879, and Gladys in 1883.

In 1886, George suffered an unspecified breakdown and the family moved to London where, once he had recovered sufficiently, they opened another boys' school, where Nelly delighted in staging 'theatricals'. She put to good use the linguistic skills she had acquired during her time in France, giving French lessons to George's pupils; she seems also to have been responsible for the translation into English of a guide to the Zermatt area by distinguished Swiss scientist Emile Yung, published in Geneva in 1894.[9]

When George was advised to give up intellectual work on health grounds, the family moved to Calcot, near Reading, where they acquired a share in a market garden. Later, Nelly's sisters Fanny and Maria came to join them for a while. In 1901, Nelly sold the lease on the house at Ampthill Square that Dickens had procured for the Ternan girls over forty years earlier, probably to help finance her son's army career; for this at least she had cause to be grateful to Dickens.

While she still lived in Margate, Nelly reportedly admitted to the local parish priest, William Benham, that she had indeed been Dickens's mistress and that he did acquire the house for her, where he visited a couple of times a week. She also confided that she had 'come to feel remorse about her relations with him during his lifetime, and that her remorse had made them both miserable; and that she now "loathed the very thought of this intimacy".[10] In 1897, Benham in turn confided this information to biographer Thomas Wright, who refrained from publishing it, at Georgy's request, until 1834 when all Dickens's children were dead, at which time he revealed it in a newspaper article, following it up in more detail in his life of Dickens in 1935.

When her sisters moved to Southsea, Nelly and George followed them to the south coast town, near Dickens's birthplace, where they all lived in circumstances of straitened gentility. After the death of Maria and then George, Fanny took Nelly into her home where, poor but spirited and now in their seventies, the sisters amused themselves by writing plays. Fanny died in 1913 and was buried with Maria.

Nelly died in 1914. Dickens's last love was laid to rest alongside her husband in the cemetery at Southsea, the same graveyard where Maria Beadnell, Dickens's first love, was buried in an unmarked grave some eighteen years before. [11]

It was the opinion of Katey Dickens that whether her father had married Maria Beadnell or Nelly Ternan, 'the ultimate result would have been the same'.

The sense of longing that haunted him throughout his life would never have left him. Charles Dickens would always have wanted more.

Chronology

1812   Born in Portsmouth to John (1785–1851) and
        Elizabeth Dickens (1789–1863), their second child
        after Frances ('Fanny', 1810–48).

1817   After short time in London, the Dickens family
        moves to Chatham, near Rochester, Kent. These were
        Dickens's happiest years.

1822   Family moves back to London.

1823   Mother fails in attempt to open a school.

1824   Charles, aged twelve, is sent to work in Warren's
        Blacking Warehouse near the Strand. Father
        imprisoned for debt at the Marshalsea prison. Wife
        and children join him except for Charles, who goes
        into lodgings, and Fanny, a resident pupil at the new
        music academy.

1825   Enrolled at Wellington House Academy.

1827–9 Works as legal clerk and freelance shorthand
        reporter at the ecclesiastical and family courts known
        as Doctors' Commons.

1830   Becomes infatuated with Maria Beadnell
        (1811–86).

1831   Begins working for *The Mirror of Parliament*, a

	weekly record of debates founded and edited by his uncle, John Barrow.
1832	Misses audition at the Covent Garden Theatre through illness. Interest and close involvement in staging 'theatricals' remains strong throughout his life.
1833	Relationship with Beadnell ends. First story published.
1834	Meets Catherine (1816–79), daughter of George Hogarth, editor of the new *Evening Chronicle*, to which Dickens contributes sketches. Sketches under pen-name 'Boz' begin to appear in the *Monthly Magazine*. Moves to chambers at Furnival's Inn. Publication begins of *The Pickwick Papers* (20 monthly instalments).
1836	Marries Catherine Hogarth.
1837	Birth of first child (Charles Culliford Boz, 'Charley'). Publication begins of *Oliver Twist* (24 monthly instalments) Moves to house in Doughty Street (now the Dickens Museum). Sister-in-law Mary Hogarth, 17, dies in his arms.
1838	Catherine suffers a miscarriage. Birth of second child (Mary, 'Mamey'). Publication begins of *Nicholas Nickleby* (20 monthly instalments).
1839	Birth of third child (Katherine Elizabeth Macready, 'Katey'). Moves to Devonshire Terrace, Regent's Park.

1840	Publication begins of *The Old Curiosity Shop* (40 weekly instalments).
1841	Birth of fourth child (Walter Landor).
	Publication begins of *Barnaby Rudge* (42 weekly instalments).
1842	First visit to America (January to June), accompanied by Catherine, leaving the children at home in care of family and friends.
	Publication begins of *Martin Chuzzlewit* (20 monthly instalments).
1843	Catherine's sister Georgina (1827–1917) joins the household.
	A Christmas Carol published.
1844	Birth of fifth child (Francis Jeffrey, 'Frank').
1844–5	Spends year on the Continent, mainly in Italy, Switzerland and France with Catherine and family.
1845	Birth of sixth child (Alfred D'Orsay Tennyson).
1846	Publication begins of *Dombey and Son* (seven monthly instalments).
1847	Birth of seventh child (Sydney Smith Haldimand).
	Begins collaboration with Angela Burdett-Coutts on the Urania Cottage project for fallen women.
1848	Death of favourite sister, Fanny, probably from tuberculosis.
1849	Birth of eighth child (Henry Fielding Charles, 'Harry').
1850	Publication begins of *David Copperfield* (19 monthly instalments).
	Launch of the journal *Household Words*.
	Birth of ninth child (Dora Annie).
1851	Death of Dora and of Dickens's father, John, within

two weeks of each other; illness of Catherine
Dickens.

Publication begins of *Bleak House* (18 monthly
instalments).

1852   Moves from Devonshire Terrace to Tavistock House.
Birth of tenth child (Edward Bulwer Lytton, 'Plorn').
In Italy and Switzerland with Wilkie Collins and
Augustus Egg.

1853   Gives first public reading, of *A Christmas Carol.*

1854   Publication begins of *Hard Times* (18 weekly
instalments).

1855   Renews acquaintance with Maria Winter (née
Beadnell).

More public readings.

1856   Publication of *Little Dorrit* begins (18 monthly
instalments).

Buys Gad's Hill Place near Rochester, a house
admired since childhood.

1857   Meets his future mistress, actress Ellen ('Nelly')
Ternan, during auditions for a Manchester perfor-
mance of *The Frozen Deep*, co-authored with Wilkie
Collins.

Publishes, in *Household Words*, 'The Lazy Tour of
Two Idle Apprentices', an account of a walking tour
with Wilkie Collins in the north of England after
meeting Ternan.

1858   Separation from Catherine.

'Personal statement' appears in *The Times* and
Household Words.

Founds the journal *All the Year Round.*

Second reading tour (14 dates).

1859   Publication begins of *A Tale of Two Cities* (28 weekly instalments).

1860   Acquires lease on Houghton House, Ampthill Square, for Nelly Ternan's sisters – it is transferred to her the following year.

Moves from London to Gad's Hill Place, but lives at various places in England and France with Ternan until his death.

Publication begins of *Great Expectations* (33 weekly instalments).

Katey Dickens marries Wilkie Collins's brother, Charles, to Dickens's dismay.

1861   Sydney, aged 13, becomes a naval cadet.

Third extensive reading tour throughout the UK (46 dates).

1862–3   Often in France with Ternan, Mamey and Georgina Hogarth.

1863   Death of mother Elizabeth, and of son Walter in India.

1864   Son Alfred emigrates to Australia.

Publication begins of *Our Mutual Friend* (18 monthly instalments).

1865   Returning from France, Dickens, Ternan and her mother are involved in the Staplehurst rail crash.

1866   Ternan's sister Fanny marries Anthony Trollope's brother Tom, and makes her home in Florence.

1867–8   Second reading tour in America (75 readings).

Abandons initial hope that Ternan might join him.

1868   Installs Ternan at Windsor Lodge, Peckham.

Youngest son Edward follows his brother Alfred to Australia.

1869	UK farewell reading tour broken off because of serious illness.
1870	Farewell reading programme in London (12 sessions).
	Publication begins of *The Mystery of Edwin Drood* (six monthly instalments, unfinished).
	After a series of minor strokes, Dickens dies at Gad's Hill Place of a brain haemorrhage on 9 June.
	Buried privately in Poets' Corner, Westminster Abbey, on 14 June.

Notes

Notes on Forward

1 Ada Nisbet, *Dickens & Ellen Ternan* (Berkeley, 1952), p. vii.
2 Nisbet, *Dickens & Ellen Ternan*, p. ix.
3 John Forster, *The Life of Charles Dickens* (London, 1874), p. 699.
4 Michael Slater, *Dickens and Women* (Yale, 2009).

Notes on Introduction

1 John Forster, *The Life of Charles Dickens* (London, 1874), p. 920. The book is dedicated 'To the daughters of Charles Dickens, my goddaughter Mary and her sister Kate … by their father's friend and executor'.
2 Quoted in Gladys Storey, *Dickens and Daughter* (London, 1939), p. 134.

Notes on Chapter 1

1 No dance was reported in the local press for 6 February 1812. The closest was on 3 February.
2 The name was misspelled as 'Huffham' in the baptismal register.
3 For a full review of the evidence, see John Bowen, 'John Dickens's birth announcements and Charles Dickens's sisters', *Dickensian*, 470, vol. 105, 3, Winter 2009, pp. 197–201.
4 John Forster, *The Life of Charles Dickens* (London 1874), p. 31.
5 Forster, *Dickens*, p. 32.
6 Forster, *Dickens*, p. 34.
7 Forster, *Dickens*, p. 32.
8 Forster, *Dickens*, p. 34.
9 Forster, *Dickens*, p. 25.
10 Forster, *Dickens*, p. 28.
11 Forster, *Dickens*, p. 28.

12 Forster, *Dickens*, p. 34.

13 Forster, *Dickens*, p. 35.

14 Forster, *Dickens*, p. 35.

15 Forster, *Dickens*, p. 35.

16 Gladys Storey, *Dickens and Daughter* (London, 1939), p. 124.

17 From a fragment of an essay from November 1889, quoted in Dan H. Laurence and Martin Quinn, eds, *Shaw on Dickens* (New York, 1985), p.7.

18 Laurence and Quinn, *Shaw on Dickens*, p.7.

19 Robert Langton, *The Childhood and Youth of Dickens* (London, 1891), p. 26.

20 Michael Slater, *Dickens and Women* (London, 1983), p. 25.

21 Slater, *Dickens and Women*, p. 25.

22 Slater, *Dickens and Women*, p. 5.

23 Forster, *Life of Dickens*, p. 36

24 Carolyn Dever, *Death and the Mother from Dickens to Freud* (Cambridge, 1998), p. 26

25 Dever, *Death and the Mother*, p. 26

26 Laurence and Quinn, *Shaw on Dickens*, p. 7

Notes on Chapter 2

1 Apparently because all advocates were required to be Oxbridge graduates.

2 Dexter, *The Love Romance*, p. 37.

3 Dexter, *The Love Romance*, p. 50–1.

4 It is interesting that Dickens calls on Goldsmith, one of his early literary inspirations. Another of Goldsmith's famous quotations, also from *Retaliation*, refers to the duplicity of the acting profession that Dickens so admired and embraced: 'On stage he was natural, simple, affecting,/Twas only when he was off, he was acting'.

5 Dexter, *The Love Romance*, pp. 28–40.

Notes on Chapter 3

1 F. G Kitton, *Dickens by Pen and Pencil*, quoted in Walter Dexter, ed., *Mr and Mrs Charles Dickens – His Letters to Her* (London, 1935).

2 The first occurred after the death of her sister Mary in 1837; the second in late December 1847, on the train from Glasgow to Edinburgh, just eight months after the birth of Sydney, and shortly before Henry's birth.

3 In America in 1867, he confided to his host and publisher James Ticknor Fields his 'deep unhappiness … in having so many children by a wife who was totally uncongenial'. George Curry, 'Charles Dickens and Annie Fields', *Huntington Library Quarterly*, vol. 51, Winter 1988, p. 9.

4 Gladys Storey, *Dickens and Daughter* (London, 1939), p. 93.

5 On 23 October 1888, Gladstone received from American physician Henry Sterling Pomeroy a copy of his newly published *Ethics of Marriage*. On reading it, he was appalled to discover the apparent extent of birth control in America. His daughter Mary, who, as his secretary, had passed the book on, recorded his reaction:

> Never as long as I live shall I forget the sight that met my eyes as I entered the room. My father was standing in an attitude of profound dejection by the fire, his head bowed, his face tragic. 'Mazy dear,' he said, 'you have dealt me one of the greatest blows of my life.' He then spoke most seriously and solemnly of the perils that beset the subject. 'If I were only twenty years younger,' he said (he was then eighty-four), his eyes flashing, his whole frame upright and alert, 'I would fight. I would head a crusade.'

Quoted in Anne Isba, *Gladstone and Women* (London, 2006), pp. 145–6.

6 Mary Scott Hogarth took her middle name from the great poet and novelist, Sir Walter Scott (1771–1832). Scott, who did so much to raise the status of the novel as a literary form, and of the novelist as a professional, was an intimate friend of George Hogarth, who at one time acted as his legal adviser; Scott also had a profound influence on Dickens's early work.

7 Now the Dickens Museum.

8 This was just six years before precisely that scenario was consummated in Emily Bronte's *Wuthering Heights*.

9 The reality was something different. The children were much more disturbed by their parents' absence than either Dickens or Catherine anticipated, and had been miserable in the care of the stern Macreadys. See Lillian Nayder, *The Other Dickens – A Life of Catherine Hogarth* (Ithaca, New York, 2010), p. 121.

10 Pilgrim 3, xi.

11 The United States decline to sign up to the International Copyright Act of 1844, and it was 1896 before the American Congress finally voted to join the International Copyright Union, ending copyright piracy.

12 Paul Schlicke, ed., *The Oxford Reader's Companion to Dickens* (Oxford, 1999), p. 375.

13 This is the autobiographical 'fragment' about his very early life, including his months at the blacking warehouse, that appear in John Forster's *Life of Dickens*.

14 Dickens seemed particularly keen to dispatch his sons in the years around and after the marriage break-up. Within the space of eight years, five of them left for distant parts of the Empire, the armed forces, or both. Walter joined the Army and, in 1857, aged sixteen, went to India (where he died

six years later). Frank joined the Bengal Mounted Police in 1864, aged twenty. In 1865, Alfred left for Australia, aged twenty. Edward followed him in 1868, aged sixteen. Sydney joined the Navy as a cadet in 1860 at the age of thirteen, very little older than Dickens had been when he first went to work at Warren's Blacking Warehouse.

15 Annie Fields, wife of Dickens's Boston publisher, recorded Dickens's 'habitual abstemiousness' in her diary, noting also that he had confided in her husband that he believed that 'nine out of ten of the bases of disagreement in marriage came from drink'. 'He is a man who has suffered evidently', she wrote, the clear implication being that Catherine Dickens drank. George Curry, 'Charles Dickens and Annie Fields', *Huntington Library Quarterly*, vol. 51, Winter 1988, p. 13.

16 Gladys Storey, *Dickens and Daughter* (London, 1939), pp. 93–4.

17 There was some suspicion that Georgy, jealous at the thought of Nelly, might have alerted Catherine to the gift of jewellery. Certainly, when the ménage moved to France, where Nelly was installed, Georgy appeared to suffer for some time from a non-specific illness, described as a heart condition, but more likely a form of depression at being upstaged.

18 Even if he and Catherine had divorced, Dickens would have been unable to marry Georgy, had he wanted to. The 1835 Marriage Act absolutely forbade marriage between siblings-in-law, even when widowed. Under Catholic and Anglican Canon Law at the time, a man and his wife became 'one flesh' on marriage; to marry a former wife's sister would therefore be incest. The topic was much debated until the Deceased Wife's Sister's Act of 1907.

19 Gladys Storey, *Dickens and Daughter* (London, 1939), p. 219.

20 Storey, *Dickens and Daughter*, pp. 22–3.

21 In fact, this was Charley Dickens's own decision.

22 Storey, *Dickens and Daughter*, p. 96.

23 Storey, *Dickens and Daughter*, p. 105.

24 Storey, *Dickens and Daughter*, p. 106.

Notes on Chapter 4

1 Marguerite, Countess of Blessington (1789–1849), was twice widowed and living with her step-daughter's estranged husband Alfred, Count d'Orsay, when Dickens first met her in 1836. Their ménage at Gore House, Kensington (now the site of the Albert Hall) was shunned by polite society, but artists and literati flocked to her extravagant salons. It was at Lady Blessington's salons that Dickens first met the poet Walter Savage Landor, who became godfather to Dickens's son Walter; the novelist Edward Bulwer-Lytton, who became his good friend and after whom

his son Edward was named; the distinguished actor William Charles Macready, who stood godfather to Dickens's daughter Katey; William Harrison Ainsworth, who became his friend, lawyer and publisher; and the Danish writer of fairy tales, Hans Christian Andersen.

2 Mention should also be made of Dickens's relationship with the novelist Elizabeth Gaskell (1810–65), particularly since it reflects his ambivalent attitude to a strong middle-class woman with a mind of her own. In the early days of their acquaintance, Dickens called her his 'Scheherazade', after the legendary storyteller in *The Arabian Nights*: 'I am sure your powers of narrative can never be exhausted by a single night, but must be good for at least a thousand nights and one.' He regarded her as his female counterpart as a writer. Impressed by her novel *Mary Barton*, which was published in 1848, he invited her to write something for the inaugural issue of the journal *Household Words* which he founded in 1850. Her initial contribution was the tale of a prostitute, 'Lizzie Leigh and a Dark Night's Work', and she rapidly became one of Dickens's major contributors. Of over forty stories and articles written by Gaskell between 1850 and her death in 1865, two-thirds were published by Dickens in *Household Words* and its successor, *All the Year Round*. However, what began as a warm professional friendship became increasingly prickly with time. Initially, this was because Gaskell feared Dickens might steal ideas from her industrial novel *North and South* (1855) for his own *Hard Times*; later, it was because of a clash of personalities over the details of his production of her work ('If I were Mr Gaskell, O heaven how I should beat her,' Dickens wrote to his colleague Harry Wills). Finally, the relationship foundered because she shared the public's 'well-grounded feeling of dislike to the publicity he has given to his domestic affairs' following the break-up of Dickens's marriage in 1858.

3 Francis Burdett to Angela, Bodleian Ms, Eng Lett., d. 98, f. 147.

4 Edna Healey, *Lady Unknown – The Life of Angela Burdett-Coutts* (London, 1978), p. 66.

5 At the time, John and Elizabeth Dickens were living in a cottage in the village of Alphington, near Exeter, which Dickens had rented for them in a short-lived attempt to get them out of London and away from embarrassing him, after once more having had to settle their debts, as he also frequently did for his 'rasping' brothers, Frederick and Augustus.

6 Healey, *Lady Unknown*, pp. 90–1.

7 Healey, *Lady Unknown*, p. 89.

8 For a comprehensive history of the project and what became of its inmates, see Jenny Hartley, *Charles Dickens and The House of Fallen Women* (London, 2008).

9 By comparison, a 2004 Home Office report gave a figure for sex workers in the entire UK as 80,000 – the same as Mayhew's estimate for Victorian London.

10 Henry Mayhew, *London Labour and the London Poor* (London, 1985), p. 259

11 See Michael Rose, ed., *The Poor and the City: the English Poor Law in its Urban Context, 1834–1914* (Leicester, 1985).

12 For the background to William Gladstone's prostitute rescue work, see Anne Isba, *Gladstone and Women* (London, 2006), Chapter 6, 'Fallen Women'.

13 James Greenwood, *The Seven Curses of London* (Oxford, 1981), p. 173. First published 1869. The other six 'curses' were neglected children, professional thieves, beggars and vagabonds, drunkenness, gambling and a waste of charity.

14 Mayhew, *London Labour,* p. xxxvi.

15 Mayhew, *London Labour,* p. *xxxv.*

16 Ibid.

17 Ibid.

18 After his recall from Van Diemen's Land, Sir John Franklin was the leader of the ill-fated Arctic expedition that inspired the play *The Frozen Deep*, co-written by Dickens and Wilkie Collins, during auditions for which Dickens first met Ellen Ternan.

19 Some referrals to Urania Cottage came from the Elizabeth Fry Refuge in Hackney, a half-way house for recently released female prisoners. The hostel was established in 1849 as her memorial. See Anne Isba, *The Excellent Mrs Fry – Unlikely Heroine* (London, 2010), pp. 196–7.

20 A post from which Maconochie was later, unjustly, dismissed.

21 The occasional emigrant went to Canada, and South Africa was the destination for one of Urania Cottage's solid success stories, Louisa Cooper. It was also to South Africa that Dickens and Miss Coutts helped a case referred to them by Elizabeth Gaskell in 1850. Gaskell, whose first contribution to Dickens's *Household Words* was 'Lizzie Leigh', the archetypal story of a 'fallen woman', had been visiting a young woman who was about to be released from Manchester's New Bailey prison. She was the sixteen-year-old orphaned daughter of a clergyman, seduced by a prison surgeon and reduced to drink and theft, but she aspired 'to redeem herself'. Family funds were available for her emigration, but Gaskell was concerned about her being 'exposed to corruption' on the outward voyage. Dickens and Coutts secured for her a passage to the Cape, and protectors for her time in London before the sailing and on the boat.

22 Alan Brooke and David Brandon, *Bound for Botany Bay – British Convict*

Voyages to Australia (London, 2005), p. 13. This book provides a comprehensive history of transportation.

23 Isba, *The Excellent Mrs Fry*, Chapter 6, 'Exiles to a distant land'.

24 For a fuller account of Alfred and Edward's time in Australia, see Thomas Keneally, 'Dickens Down Under', *Observer* (London, 7 November 2010). Also, Dickens himself was interested in the thought of visiting Australia. In 1862, he was offered £10,000 for an eight-month reading tour down under. But the distance was so far – the boat took two to three months in each direction – and the thought of being away from Nelly for so long was intolerable.

25 The case study book appears not to have survived. It may have been among the accumulated letters and papers of twenty years that Dickens consigned to a bonfire of the vanities at Gad's Hill in September 1860. 'As it was an exquisite day when I began, and rained very heavily when I finished, I suspect my correspondence of having overcast the face of the Heavens.'

26 The drying equipment gave 'great satisfaction', according to sanitation reformer Dr John Sutherland (1801–91) who headed a commission sent out to Crimea to report on the sanitary conditions of British soldiers.

27 Miss Coutts and Dr and Mrs Brown were holidaying in Montpellier when Brown died. His wife being incapacitated by grief, Dickens stepped in and made all the arrangements to have the body brought back to London for the funeral, which he also organized.

28 Healey, *Lady Unknown*, p. 136.

29 Hartley, *The House of Fallen Women*, p. 245.

Notes on Chapter 5

1 For the full significance of the Manchester Art Treasures Exhibition, see Christopher Hodkinson, *A Question of Attribution: the Evolution of Connoisseurship During the Nineteenth Century*, unpublished PhD thesis (Lancaster University, 2009), Chapter 3, 'A New Narrative and a Great Display', *passim*.

2 One diary, for January to November 1867, survived because it was lost or stolen in December while Dickens was in New York. It resurfaced at an auction there in 1922, the property of an 'unnamed private collector'.

3 Claire Tomalin, *The Invisible Woman: The Story of Nelly Ternan and Charles Dickens* (London, 1990), pp. 147–8.

4 Pilgrim, 1865, p. 53.

5 Pilgrim, 1865, p. 56–7. The manuscript in question was instalment 16 of *Our Mutual Friend*.

6 The first Divorce Act became law in 1857. Previously, divorces had

required an Act of Parliament. Even with the new law, of which a sister-in-law of his took advantage, Dickens would have been unable to divorce Catherine except for adultery.

7 Tomalin, *The Invisible Woman*, p. 144.

8 George Curry, 'Charles Dickens and Annie Fields', *Huntington Library Quarterly*, vol. 51, Winter 1988, p. 44.

9 M. A. de Wolfe Howe, *Memories of a Hostess* (Boston, 1922), p. 168.

10 Gladys Storey, *Dickens and Daughter* (London, 1939), p. 136.

11 Storey, *Dickens and Daughter*, p. 134.

12 Storey, *Dickens and Daughter*, p. 136.

13 Storey, *Dickens and Daughter*, p. 136.

14 Storey, *Dickens and Daughter*, p. 138.

15 John Forster, *The Life of Charles Dickens* (London, 1874), p. 945.

16 When the Duke of Wellington died in September 1852, Dickens wrote to Miss Coutts after the funeral denouncing the 'barbarous show and expense' of state funerals. Two months later, he wrote a piece entitled 'Trading in Death' for *Household Words*, quoting a large number of advertisements that had appeared in *The Times* newspaper, offering seats to view the funeral, autographs and locks of Wellington's hair.

17 Forster, *Life*, p. 952.

18 *The Times*, June 15 1870, p. 12.

19 For a comprehensive forensic analysis of whether Nelly Ternan was likely to have been present at Dickens's funeral, see Robert Garnett, 'The Mysterious Mourner – Dickens's Funeral and Ellen Ternan', *Dickens Quarterly*, vol. 25, June 2008, pp. 107–18.

20 Tomalin, *The Invisible Woman*, p. 189.

21 Forster, *Life*, p. 952.

22 Forster, *Life*, p. 949.

23 Forster, *Life*, p. 951.

Notes on Chapter 6

1 For a comprehensive account of Catherine Dickens's social life after the separation from her husband, see Lillian Nayder, *The Other Dickens – A Life of Catherine Hogarth* (Ithaca, New York, 2010), pp. 288–95.

2 Gladys Storey, *Dickens and Daughter* (London, 1939), p. 164.

3 Dan H. Laurence and Martin Quinn, eds, *Shaw on Dickens* (New York, 1985), p. xix.

4 Laurence and Quinn, *Shaw on Dickens*, p. xix.

5 Claire Tomalin, *The Invisible Woman – The Story of Nelly Ternan and Charles Dickens* (London, 1990), p. 228.

6 Healey, *Lady Unknown*, p. 191.

7   Healey, *Lady Unknown*, p. 226.

8   In fact, in the 1881 census, she gave her age as twenty-eight, a staggering fourteen years less than the truth. Tomalin, *The Invisible Woman*, p. 220.

9   John Bowen, 'Acts of Translation', *Times Literary Supplement*, 5457, 2 November 2007, p. 14.

10   Tomalin, *The Invisible Woman*, p. 231.

11   Michael Slater, *Dickens and Women* (London, 1983), p. 76.

Bibliography

Ackroyd, Peter, *Dickens* (London, 1990).

Adrian, Arthur, *Georgina Hogarth and the Dickens Circle* (London, 1957).

Allen, Michael, *Charles Dickens' Childhood* (Basingstoke, 1988).

Begley, Louis, *The Tremendous World I Have Inside My Head – Franz Kafka, a Biographical Essay* (New York, 2008).

Bentley, Nicolas, Slater, Michael and Burgis, Nina, *The Dickens Index* (Oxford, 1990).

Bodenheimer, Rosemarie, *Knowing Dickens* (Cornell, 2007).

Bowen, John, *Other Dickens* (Oxford, 2000).

— 'Bebelle and "His Boots"; Dickens, Ellen Ternan and the Christmas Stories', *Dickensian*, vol. 96, 3, Winter 2000, pp. 197–208.

— 'Acts of Translation', *Times Literary Supplement* 5457 (London, 2007), p. 14.

— 'John Dickens's birth announcements and Charles Dickens's sisters', *Dickensian*, 470, vol. 105, 3, Winter 2009, pp. 197–201.

Brooke, Alan and Brandon, David, *Bound for Botany Bay – British Convict Voyages to Australia* (London, 2005).

Collins, Philip, 'Dickens and his Readers' in *Victorian Values*

– *Personalities and Perspectives in Nineteenth Century Society*, ed. Gordon Marsden (London, 1990), pp. 42–57.

Curry, George, 'Charles Dickens and Annie Fields', *Huntington Library Quarterly*, vol. 51, Winter 1988.

Dever, Carolyn, *Death and the Mother from Dickens to Freud: Victorian Fiction and the Anxiety of Origins* (Cambridge, 2006).

DeWolfe Howe, M. A, *Memories of a Hostess* (Boston, 1922).

Dickens, Charles, *Letters*, House, M. and Storey, G., eds, 12 vols. (Oxford, 1965). The Pilgrim edition.

Dexter, Walter, ed., *Dickens to his Oldest Friend – The Letters of a Lifetime from Charles Dickens to Thomas Beard* (London, 1932).

— *The Love Romance of Charles Dickens (Told in his Letters to Maria Beadnell)* (London, 1936).

Forster, John, *The Life of Charles Dickens* (London, n.d., 1874?).

Fry, Elizabeth, *Observations on the Visiting, Superintendence and Government of Female Prisoners* (London, 1827).

Garnett, Robert R., 'The crisis of 1863', *Dickens Quarterly*, Sept 2006.

— 'The mysterious mourner: Dickens's funeral and Ellen Ternan', *Dickens Quarterly*, June 2008.

Gaskell, Elizabeth, *Lizzie Leigh and a Dark Night's Work* (Stroud, 2008), first published 2008.

Gearing, Nigel, *Dickens in America* (London, 1998).

Hardwick, Michael and Mollie, eds, *The Charles Dickens Encyclopaedia* (London, 1973).

Hartley, Jenny, *Charles Dickens and the House of Fallen Women* (London, 2008).

Hawksley, Lucinda, *Katey – the Life and Loves of Dickens's Artist Daughter* (London, 2006).

Healey, Edna, *Lady Unknown – the Life of Angela Burdett-Coutts* (London, 1978).

Hodkinson, Christopher, 'A Question of Attribution – the Evolution of Connoisseurship During the Nineteenth Century', unpublished PhD thesis (Lancaster University, 2009).

House, Humphry, *The Dickens World* (Oxford, 1941).

Ingham, Patricia, *Dickens, Women and Language* (New York, 1992).

Isba, Anne, *Gladstone and Women* (London, 2006).

— *The Excellent Mrs Fry – Unlikely Heroine* (London, 2010).

Johnson, Edgar, ed., *Letters from Charles Dickens to Angela Burdett-Coutts, 1841–1865* (London, 1953).

Keneally, Thomas,' Dickens Down Under', *The Observer*, 7 November 2010.

Langton, Robert, *The Childhood and Youth of Charles Dickens* (London, 1891).

Laurence, Dan H. and Quinn, Martin, eds, *Shaw on Dickens* (New York, 1985).

Nayder, Lillian, *The Other Dickens – A Life of Catherine Hogarth* (Ithaca, New York, 2010).

Nisbet, Ada, *Dickens & Ellen Ternan* (Berkeley, 1952).

Pope, Norris, *Dickens and Charity* (London, 1978).

Pope-Hennessy, Una, *Charles Dickens* (London, 1945).

Rose, William, ed. *The Poor and the City – The English Poor Law and its Urban Context, 1834–1914* (Leicester, 1985).

Schlicke, Paul, *The Oxford Reader's Companion to Dickens* (Oxford, 1999).

Schor, Hilary, *Dickens and the Daughter of the House* (Cambridge, 2007).

Slater, Michael, *Dickens and Women* (London, 1983).

— *Dickens* (Yale, 2009).

Storey, Gladys, *Dickens and Daughter* (London, 1939).

Tomalin, Claire, *The Invisible Woman – the Story of Nelly Ternan and Charles Dickens* (London, 1990).

Uglow, Jenny, *Elizabeth Gaskell* (London, 1993).

Waters, Catherine, *Dickens and the Politics of the Family* (Cambridge 1997).

Acknowledgements

I should like to express my gratitude first of all to Continuum's publishing director, Robin Baird-Smith, who suggested to me the subject of this book; and to Dickens specialist Professor John Bowen and nineteenth-century social historian Professor David Vincent for helping ensure the idea took flight. Professor Bowen also generously suggested various avenues of enquiry that I might otherwise have missed.

Historian friends the Venerable Bill Pritchard and Dr Josephine Wilkinson kept me going whenever the creative process threatened to stall, as at times it must. Jo also kindly composed the index for me.

The library staff at the University of Keele were unfailingly supportive, as always; so, too, were the staff at the National Portrait Gallery; and at the Dickens Museum at Doughty House, the great man's only surviving London residence, curator Fiona Jenkins and her team could not have been more helpful. I thank them all.

I am also very grateful for the insights into the mind of Dickens provided by the published works of Peter Ackroyd, Michael Slater, Claire Tomalin and, more recently, Lillian Nayder.

Acknowledgements

A big thank-you goes also to my children Ben, Rachel, Miriam, and my friend Dr Chris Hodkinson, who kept up a level of moral support that stopped just comfortably this side of nagging. Ben also supplied invaluable additional research on an almost daily basis; Chris also read the manuscript for me. All errors, of course, remain my own.

A final vote of gratitude goes to the American friends of my childhood with whom I shared summer holidays on a small island in a New Hampshire lake, and who shared with me some transatlantic perceptions of Dickens. With nothing to do but eat, sleep, swim, listen to the loons, sit on my verandah and write about Dickens – lured on by the promise of a large gin and tonic if the daily word count was achieved before supper – I managed, as in previous years, to write at a speed unparalleled elsewhere.

Index

Index

Index

Index

Index